DAN WALSH   THE PROCESS OF PAINTING

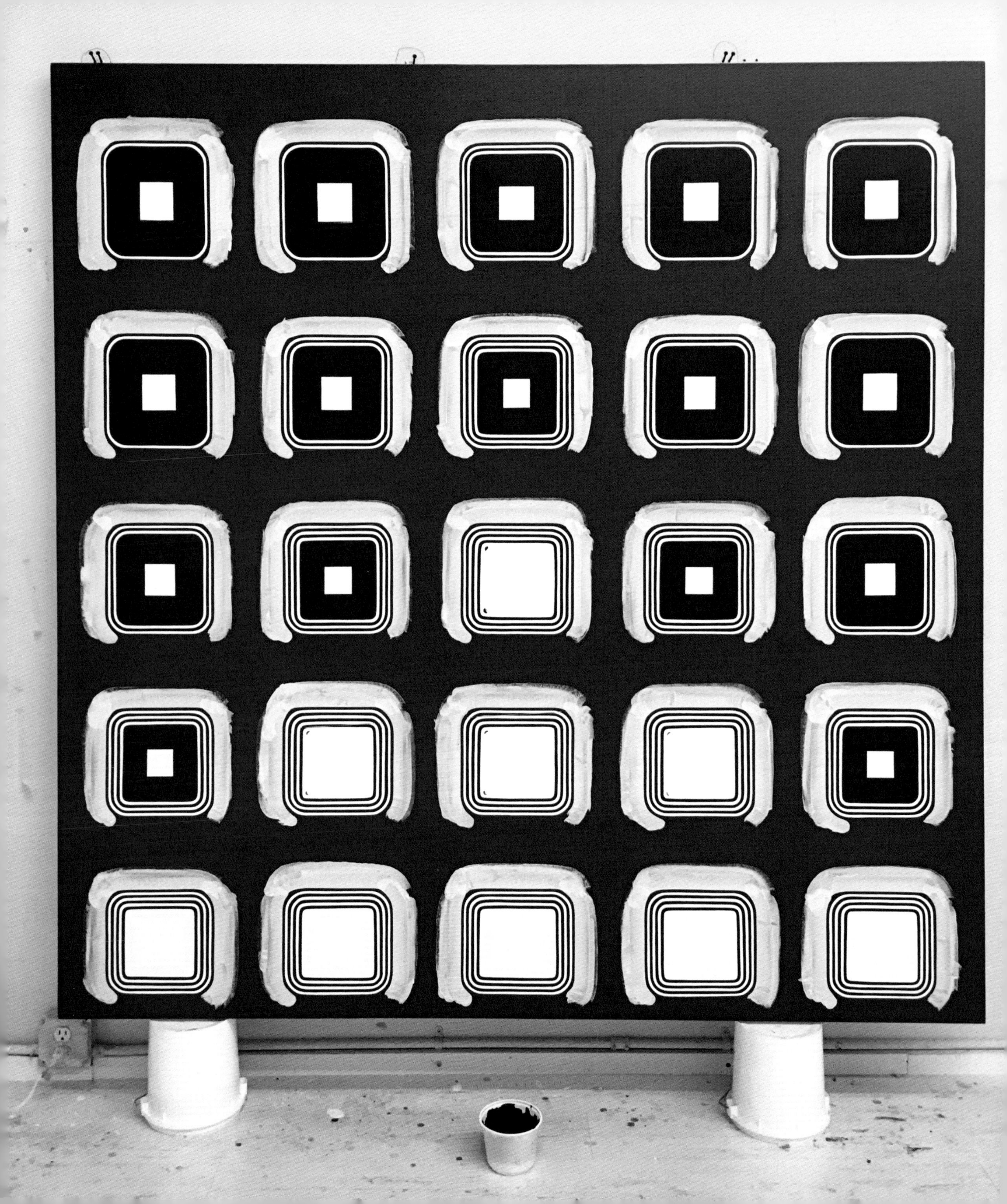

DAN WALSH
THE PROCESS OF PAINTING

jrp|editions   In collaboration with **GALERIE TSCHUDI**

Ways of Seeing / Ways of Seeking
Dan Walsh Paints a Painting

Bob Nickas

Backdrop

The stages of the painting which are reproduced on these pages illustrate arbitrarily, even haphazardly, some of the stops en route—like cities that were visited, friends that were met. They are neither better nor worse, more or less "finished," than the terminus. They are memories which the camera has changed to tangible souvenirs. Some might appear more satisfactory than the ending, but this is irrelevant. The voyage, on the other hand, is relevant: the exploration for a constantly elusive vision; the solution to a problem that was continually being set in new ways. And the ending is like the poets' ending, too; the voyage simply stops. You are not necessarily "home again"; need for the particular journey no longer exists. The result, like that of all works of art, can be compared to a new map of the human sensibility.

So wrote Thomas B. Hess in "De Kooning Paints a Picture," published in the March 1953 issue of *ARTnews*, which followed Willem de Kooning's progress, abandonment, and return to *Woman 1* (1950–1952), now in the collection of The Museum of Modern Art in New York. If Hess's phrasing and message sound conspicuously lofty to us today, his language befits a period in the New York art world characterized by existential struggle and romantic heroics. Paintings in 1952 were still referred to as pictures, a holdover from the 19th century, even at the height of abstract expressionism; in de Kooning's case, pictorial references would have been appropriate as he pursued a hybrid image, abstraction inhabited by a figure, unlike anything else exhibited then, and for a good while after. Between the early 1950s and late 1960s, *ARTnews* published many pieces in the "Paints a Picture" series, which followed the development of works by artists such as Richard Diebenkorn, Jean Dubuffet, Hans Hofmann, Alex Katz, Joan Mitchell, Jackson Pollock, Robert Rauschenberg, and Jack Tworkov. The essays were written by, among others, Lawrence Alloway, Elaine de Kooning, Frank O'Hara, Fairfield Porter, Irving Sandler, James Schuyler, and Gene Swenson. Their subjects and authors, unsurprisingly for the times, were predominantly male. Some of the writers were poets, some were artists themselves, and the pieces were at times accompanied by photographs of the artists at work in the studio. Hess, who was the editor of *ARTnews* (a position he would hold for another twenty years), was important enough for de Kooning to open the studio to him. Then as now, only insiders and allies gained entry: close friends, including other artists, curators, critics, and someone like Hess, who would go on to write a de Kooning monograph in 1959. The "Paints a Picture" series was often informed by the voices of the artists, arising from the sort of conversations that might only occur in the place where art is made and under discussion as it appears in the process of becoming. In 1965, Ad Reinhardt, iconoclast that he was, with the clever, mischievous mind of a writer, would interview himself for the series.[1] His answers to his own questions were uniformly "Yes" until the end, when he concluded with an emphatic "No." It is tempting to think of Reinhardt parodying the "Yes"/"No" interview responses of Andy Warhol in this period—an artist never chosen for "Paints a Picture"—as well as playing with the intention of the series itself: a revealing of what goes on behind the studio door, with a view to the artist's inner thoughts.

Philip Guston once famously observed, "When you're in the studio painting, there are a lot of people in there with you—your teachers, friends, painters from history, critics … and one by one if you're really painting, they walk out. And if you're really painting, you walk out." For artists, the studio may be thought of as a private world—once the door is closed, the world disappears. It is a space into which even they may disappear. And so, to be given access is a privilege. Most gallery- and museum-goers will only ever see art on the walls in its final state, fully resolved,[2] unaware that the artists among us have made themselves vulnerable, their work placed on public display, exposed to critical attention that may or may not be welcome or that overlooks the process involved, not only in terms of steps taken, but a process that is also cerebral and temporal. Was the artwork made in a day or a week, in a month or many months? Did it encompass a year? This temporality is rarely visible. A "Date Painting" by On Kawara, for example, would have been made within the space of twenty-four hours—as we can plainly see from the date inscribed—while a painting by Myron Stout might only have been considered finished after twenty-four years (*Aegis*, 1955–1979). Hours, years. Who knows where the time goes? For the viewer, art in an exhibition will present few if any signs of its passage to finalization, especially if it had been fraught, having gone through various stages and changes on its way to completion.

The "Paints a Picture" series appears intended as a means of countering the view that art on a wall is a fait accompli, already done, effortless, even inevitable, although inevitability at least implies time elapsed, a passing from one point to another. The steps in-between are mostly unseen. (In any number of paintings by Carroll Dunham there are multiple dates noted on the canvas, a timeline indicating the various stages through which an image had gone from start to finish.) In showing the evolution of a work, the *ARTnews* series, particularly at its inception, in a moment when expressive and all-over painting was prominent—possibly emphasizing the hand over the mind of the artist, in Pollock's case a form of body-operating—was also meant to heighten awareness of, and thus respect for, the artist's cerebral engagement. Action painting, so-called, was not only a matter of movement from thought to expression, but when taking in to account a work's reconsideration as the process unfolded, what may have seemed with a finished image—if it was seen as an image at all—to have been a mad dash, had in fact proceeded deliberately, mentally, and incrementally. Of course, in the 1950s and 1960s, the average museum-goer was not likely to have been a reader of *ARTnews*. Then as now, to venture into an art magazine, to do more than flip through and glance at pictures, just as being able to visit an artist's studio, is for a fairly select few. The art audience in museums has never been larger than it is today, yet despite Acoustiguide devices, guided tours, interactive displays, and wall texts—whether dumbed down or serving as apologia—the number of informed visitors, in terms of depth, is relatively small, comprised of artists, critics, curators, committed collectors, and art historians; in short, those who go beyond the surface. In recent years there has been an increasing investigation into what lies beneath an image, as infrared photography utilized in restoration has led to the discovery of underpainting, initial sketches, alterations, and so on. Visitors to galleries and museums, just as they are usually not privy to what takes place in studios, are also not involved in forensic art research. How, then, is the life of an artwork, or lives plural, known prior to its final appearance? At times this will be anecdotal, when an artist or a curator shares its narrative, or there is photographic evidence—a photograph, or a series of photographs, taken over the course of a work's development and detours, its transitions and transformations. The painter Anna Conway has occasionally reproduced a photograph of a work in an early, awkward stage as a means of showing us—and herself(?)—how an image can be wrested from uncertainty, how a composition is a matter of paring down or further articulating visual information, the clues that tell the story. In this particular painting, *It's not going to happen like that* (2013), a figure that had stood before a mirror was completely painted out, but would come to inhabit the final image nonetheless. A vanishing act? Can a person leave a painting the way they leave a room—they simply turn and walk out? Joanne Greenbaum is another artist who uses photography as she makes her way from initial steps through to a painting she considers finished. These photographs, simply snapped with a phone in the studio, allow her to see where she is going, or might go, and, looking back at them, where she has been. This is a way of seeing in addition to being present before a canvas, different to observing it with one's own eyes, because in a photograph it may appear as it would be seen by someone else, and a photograph somehow holds everything in place, the image fixedly present. Even as the phone is held in the palm of the artist's hand, there is distance.

Foreground

The novelist Émile Zola once famously remarked, "In my opinion you cannot say you have thoroughly seen anything until you have a photograph of it." This is undeniable. What Zola understood, someone born not long after photography first appeared in France, is that we comprehend spatial relations in a photograph, in its framing of space, the elimination of everything external—offering an uninterrupted view to the picture plane of the world—as nowhere else. Zola's was also a time in which it was claimed that photography had made painting obsolete. What we would come to see, long after the medium's invention, is how photography went on to make painting possible, by way of the silkscreen in the 1960s and with photorealism in the 1970s, but in general as a tool in the studio that allows the artist to follow the path taken in the act of making their work. The artists in the "Paints a Picture" series did not take their own photographs, and they may not have seen the photographs that were taken until they were published, but the process of beginnings, advancements, detours, and so on is nothing less than the history of painting to a far greater degree than perhaps any other art form. Even more than drawing, painting is always potentially under erasure—the *Erased de Kooning* drawing by Rauschenberg (1953) being the least of it. In photography, whether a picture is mechanically realized or camera-less, images are fixed once printed.[3] In printmaking, once an image is imprinted it can only be overprinted, which has its limits, added to rather than subtracted from. In sculpture, there is the possibility, after wood or stone has been carved away, to be put back where it was, though this seems only rarely done. (Ice sculpture, whether serious or decorative, as it will inevitably melt away, remains the most insistent conceptual art of all.)[4] While it is true that a sculptor may begin a work and set it aside for many years, this is a matter more related to interruption: boredom, indecision, lack of funds, other projects taking precedence, and so on. The space between the beginning and conclusion of a painting, a space in which the artist may roam around and linger in the reworking of an image, is unique among the various traditional forms of art. De Kooning's *Woman 1*, as Thomas Hess noted, was begun in early June 1950, and the artist would spend eighteen months on the painting before he abandoned it, removing the canvas from its stretcher. After a studio visit with the art historian Meyer Schapiro, who was curious to see a painting that had been cast aside, de Kooning would eventually return to it, restretch the canvas, and work on it until he was satisfied. Almost exactly two years had passed since the painting was begun. Today, when we look at *Woman 1* in the museum, we stand before a painting that might never have been.

Initially reading Hess on de Kooning, one of the artists who comes readily to mind is Dan Walsh, who has a long history of photographing his paintings as they progress in the studio—developing gradually, step-by-step—having done so since 2015. The photographs comprising this book account for twelve paintings chosen from those made over the past four years. In each case not all the photographs taken have been reproduced, only those that advance our view to his process: giving himself a starting point and seeing where it leads from day to day. He usually spends anywhere between two and six weeks on a painting, with the first photograph made within the first week. As Walsh has noted, "Something has to happen to take a picture." From this we understand that something has to change significantly enough for him to take another, and another. While the starting point for a painting may appear to have been crudely, quickly rendered, it can also appear nearly as subtly refined as the final image, as with the earliest stage of *Forge* (2020). It is tempting, in fact, to see the documented stages of this painting as a suite of seven finished prints, or a consecutive run of pages in one of the artist's handmade books. Here we grasp how printmaking, bookmaking, and the idea of an imprinted image may inform works on canvas, and how the reverse would hold true. Walsh, unique among painters of his generation, has a long, varied history with prints and books, having taught himself, and explored a wide range of techniques. When he is not in the studio painting, working toward an exhibition, it is not uncommon for his attention to turn to one or another medium. Alternating between prints, books, and paintings, and for many years now, we can appreciate how his memory of images and how they were achieved carries over from paper to the page to the canvas, and back. What he has in advance of a painting is all that he knows from what he has done, and not only on canvas. Of the book format, Walsh has observed, "It became more a place to research an idea and show the variations through a succession of images." In this we have a perfect encapsulation of the seven images, one to the next, that led to *Forge*.

Another painting that can be related to Walsh's activities parallel to painting, and to how he is able to transform humble beginnings into a resonant image, is *Call* (2022, see p. 86–91). Its earliest stage is so rudimentary—fourteen gray/blue building blocks vertically stacked, seven on each side of the canvas, short at the bottom, increasingly longer toward the top, creating a pyramidal form at the center—that the completed painting is nothing short of a revelation. About a month after he began, Walsh arrived at an image both simple and complex, unlike anything he had ever done before, at least on canvas. The image simultaneously evokes electronic circuitry and Pacific Northwest totems, technological as well as symbolic visual languages, equally encoded—his image seemingly carved to be imprinted/painted. Here we note, among Walsh's prints, a number made from woodblocks—sculptural objects in their own right—that he has exhibited from time to time. *Call*, in its pared down chromatics and "perforations," also calls to mind wood veneers that have been incised, or a template from which other images may be generated. Walsh's process, and with the various printing techniques he draws upon, acknowledge processes plural, would make him an ideal subject for the "Paints a Picture" series, were it still being done, or were it to be revived. So, too, would Philip Taaffe, an artist who, like Walsh, has incorporated printing in his painting—linoprint, silkscreen, woodblock, and monoprint—almost always involving collage compositionally, from the mid-1980s onward. Taaffe and Walsh also share an affinity for optical and ornamental imagery suggestive of non-Western cultures. Other artists whose process-oriented abstraction and step-by-step image-making would be revealed by way of sequential photography in the studio, as with "Paints a Picture," include Ellen Gallagher, Joanne Greenbaum, Charline von Heyl, Tillman Kaiser, and Sally Ross, among others. In this book there are, on average, seven photographs that tell the story of how a painting emerged. The editing of them for publication, a necessary matter of concision in relating the image as it unfolded, may be related to the creation of the paintings themselves, the fine-tuning each requires. As Walsh pursues images, teasing them out, they begin to appear to him, a holistic coming together of elements, at times as alternating currents, compositionally, chromatically. Of this he has said, "The logic of the painting reveals itself to me." The artist's way of seeing is also a way of seeking. He might not have made any of these paintings if the process was predictable. In each instance, comparing the first photograph taken with the last, even with all those in-between, we are still left to wonder, "How did he get from there to there?" Walsh very likely surprised himself as well. Hess saw de Kooning as one of those artists who "prefer to keep off balance. They insist that everything is possible within the painting, which means they must devise a system for studying an infinitely variable number of probabilities." This seems true for Walsh as well, and yet he does not have a system preordained. He has a foundation in the grid, which is not only something to build upon, as with Stanley Whitney's color-block work, but a structure to animate in unexpected ways, allowing it to perform, playfully at times, to fluctuate, optically and rhythmically, to morph and be taken, and take us, elsewhere. Despite an impression shared by any number of this artist's fans, followers, and collectors, Walsh never works from a drawing made in advance. He does not create an image to be painted, as if a painting is executed by design, color-by-numbers. Rather, the image will be drawn out slowly, progressively on the canvas itself. Counter to Hess's referencing infinite probabilities, Walsh is always hovering around and considering possibilities, open to whatever happens next. Probability refers to what is likely to occur. Walsh would not want to know in advance where the next step will take him. If this were the case, he would lose the sense of engagement that gives an artist the reason to do something else, to remain off-balance as a way of finding his footing, leading to the image's equilibrium. Some artists do have preparatory drawings, and the assistants to realize their works based on "maps" for which the most direct route will be taken—one of the reasons for the impersonal feel that accompanies this sort of production. Walsh's paintings, in contrast, as these photographs show, require his own hand, his touch, various turns and detours, a certain sensibility that is mutually manual and cerebral. Hess also refers to "a problem … continually being set in new ways." This certainly applies to Walsh's way of working, and if this is a problem, it is a good one to have.

Start to Finish, Step-By-Step

Considering a single painting from start to finish—one being sufficient to trace the moves he often makes as he finds his way with a painting—through all its iterations, with its sequence of photographs, is the best way of following the artist's process step-by-step. With *Gate* (2019, see p.15–21), appropriately enough, we have our entry point.

In its earliest stage, photographed on July 22, 2019, *Gate* barely resembles a work by Walsh. Comparing this photograph with the completed painting, in a picture taken in the studio a little over five weeks later, on August 30, we can identify in its roughed-out beginnings, a number of key elements that we associate with this artist, the grid first of all. Here, Walsh begins with a quick brushy grid of squarish forms, pale copper brown, with curved edges along the outer frame—a hallmark of his. Like a laid-back driver on a familiar looped circuit, he smoothly navigates each turn. Although his favored format is a square (55 by 55, or 70 by 70 inches), where the image meets the corners of the canvas he rounds them; most of the internal squares are rounded as well. (The only ninety-degree angles in a painting of his are the four corners of the stretched canvas.) What Walsh consistently does with the modernist grid is soften its geometry, giving it personality, movement, at times a playfulness. While there are straight edges in his paintings, all turn in and around every square, elongated rectangle, and lozenge. In this we can see something organic, the way pebbles are smoothed as they repeatedly wash upon the shore with the tide, and the long arc of the shoreline itself. Here is a reminder of the gently turned corners in the paintings of Myron Stout, who was inspired by the coast and dunes near his Provincetown studio between the 1950s and 1980s, his images countering the more rigid Minimalism that Walsh's generation of painters would absorb and rearticulate. At this early stage of *Gate* we can also identify the stylized diamonds formed at the intersections of the squares, set in what appears to be an airy white latticework.

The next day, July 23rd, at the painting's second stage, everything has been tightened up, appearing more defined yet still loosely rendered.

Later that same day, at what we will refer to as the third stage, the squares comprising the grid now have multiple rounded forms on one or two sides, internally and externally. They bump up against one another, enlivening the narrow negative space between them. Four days later, July 27th, at the painting's fourth stage, Walsh takes another picture of the painting after having heavily whitened the copper brown squares, and as lozenge forms very faintly begin to appear. He already sees them coming. The attenuated diamond and half diamond shapes that now clearly grid the painting give the canvas the feel of a large sheet of perforated paper, which would allow for individual squares to be removed, as with a sheet of stamps.

Later that day, at the fifth stage, there is a sharper definition for all the edges and curves. Chromatically, the painting is copper brown and smudged white.

Two days later, on July 29th, at the sixth stage, a pale yellow has been added, which further defines the squares, contrasting the white and brown, giving a sense of depth to the overall structure, which is increasingly imagistic.

On July 31st, at the seventh stage, a blue, somehow equally pale and bold, has been added, offering greater contrast, nuance, and depth. The blue forms now sit forward in the ground. At the eighth stage, on August 2nd, the yellow is gone, the blue forms have been pared down, and the white squares within each square have been refined.

At the ninth, on August 4th, yellow has been reintroduced to suggest a structure inside the overall structure. As we look at the construction, since this is what it is, we see yellow and white lozenge forms, some short, most long, stacked vertically and horizontally. A number of short white ones central to the composition have been set on top of longer yellow lozenges. The grid is composed of twenty-five squares. Yellow forms internally occupy a central column of five, flanked by four vertical squares on either side, having yellow elements. This structure reads as twelve squares, three by four, crowned by a thirteenth atop the center column. There are now white forms over yellow over blue over copper brown. In the movement of the image toward the viewer, and in the studio toward himself, Walsh brings this structure subtly forward. While this seems to have occurred to him as the painting was nearing the finish line, as we follow the photographs taken across a month-plus, we can see that his denouement—how various elements are brought toward resolution, a conflict's unfolding—had been playing out all along. In the last stage, leading to the painting's completion, Walsh added soft blue lozenge forms to eight of the squares that rise from the center base. He almost always anchors his image to the bottom edge of the canvas, just as he hangs his paintings low to the floor, mindful that someone will stand before them: a figure/ground relationship based on a viewer in the room. The floor beneath their feet is also immediately beneath the painting, serving to anchor the viewer within the architecture and the painting. (A wall, he might say, is not simply to be hung upon.) Walsh now had a fully discernible "steepled" structure at the center. To complete the painting, he added a small round white circle, a cue ball of sorts, to three of the five central squares, stacked as usual from the bottom up. Each white ball sits on top of two vertical blue lozenges, which are on top of three horizontal yellow lozenges, on top of four horizontal blue lozenges, over five copper lozenges, alternately horizontal and vertical, square to square. If this sounds confusing, the opposite is true: Just look at the photograph of the finished painting. His moves all cohere, and an arrival that took Walsh many weeks appears to us, in an instant, as inevitable. Clearly, it all adds up: one, two, three, four, five. Stage by stage, a process of addition and subtraction has been engaged, with the introduction, removal, and reintroduction of forms and color as he builds and reconstructs a painting, as he imagines and reimagines an image in the act of painting. All writing, it has been said, is rewriting. For Dan Walsh, within the vocabulary of his visual language, all painting is repainting. Every painting that he makes might have been another, or was, or will be.

1. Reinhardt's piece was published in the March 1965 issue of the magazine.
2. Vija Celmins has on occasion taken a painting that was in an exhibition, and may have been sold, back to the studio, not completely satisfied, wanting to continue working on it.
3. There are, of course, overpainted photographs, but these mingle two distinct mediums.

4. The earliest precedent for a serious art work utilizing ice as a material is Allan Kaprow's Happening, *Fluids* (1967, later recreated in 2008 and 2015). He had groups of volunteers build large rectangular ice block structures in various locations in and around Los Angeles in October, when the temperature was still warm—+25°C (+75°F)—accompanied by abundant sunshine, and left them to melt.

The Swiss artist Olivier Mosset, a fan of Kaprow's, created ice sculptures for exhibitions in 1994, 2019, and 2020. For this artist, the light passing through the ice, which became increasingly transparent, was also the work's material. With these ephemeral works Mosset also acknowledged one of his foundational positions on art: that it is impermanent.

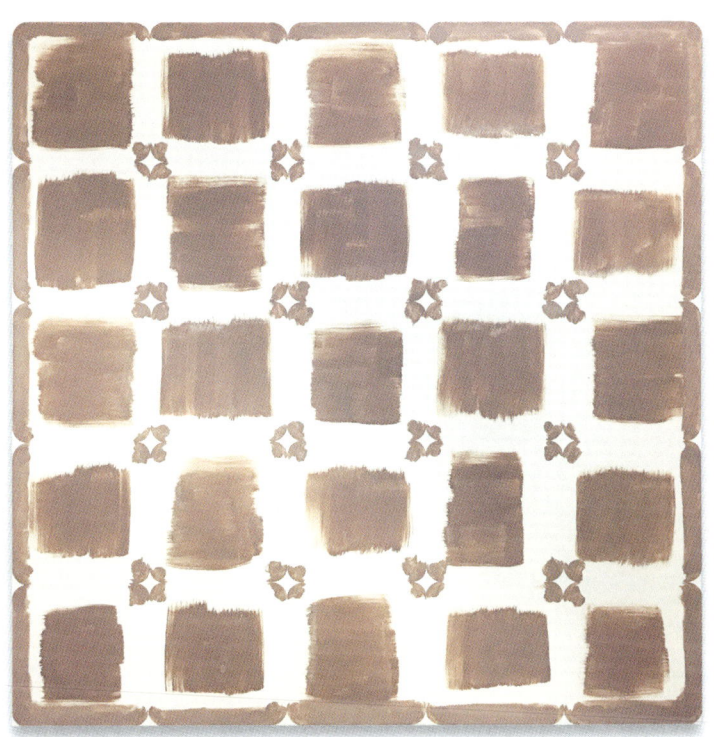

July 22, 2019

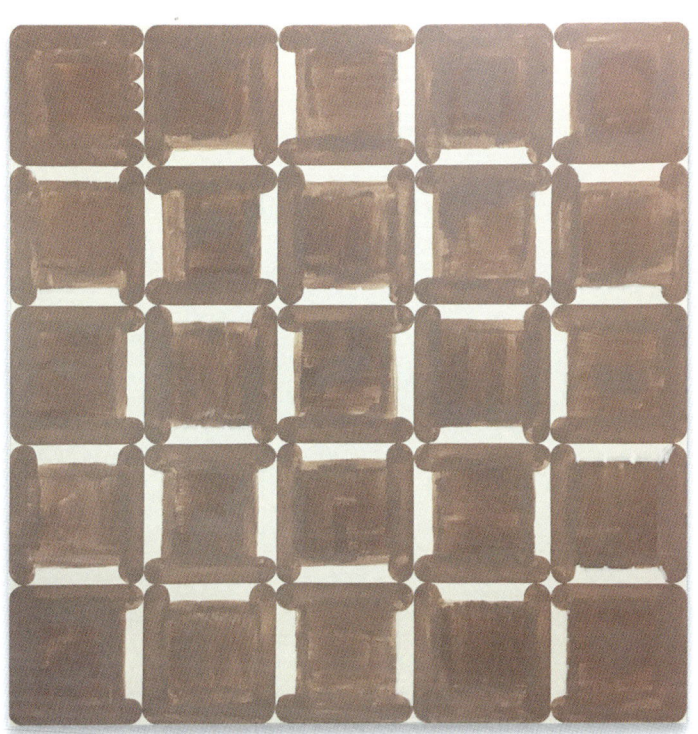

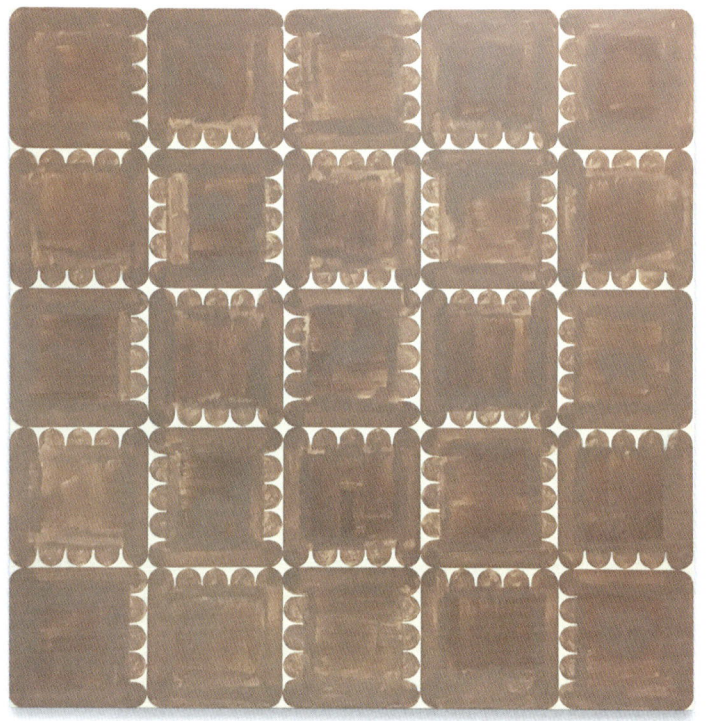
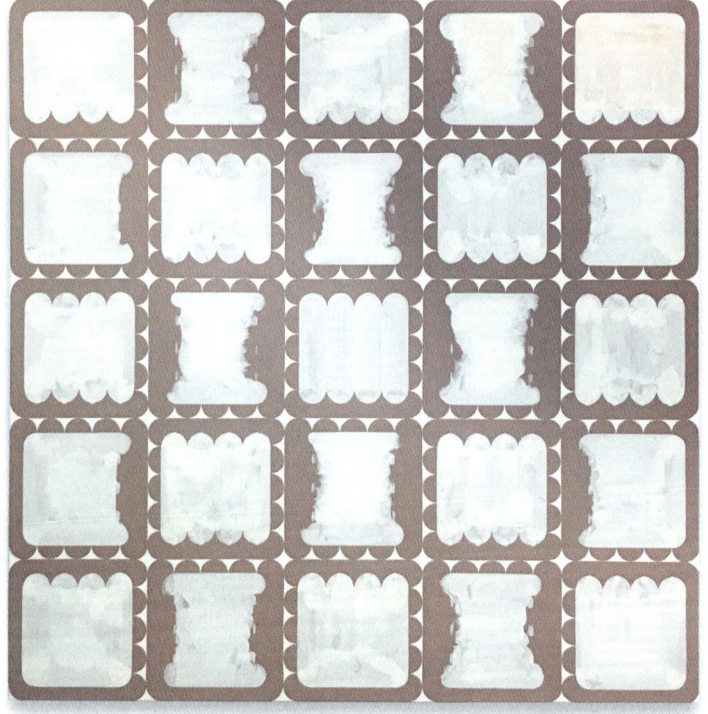

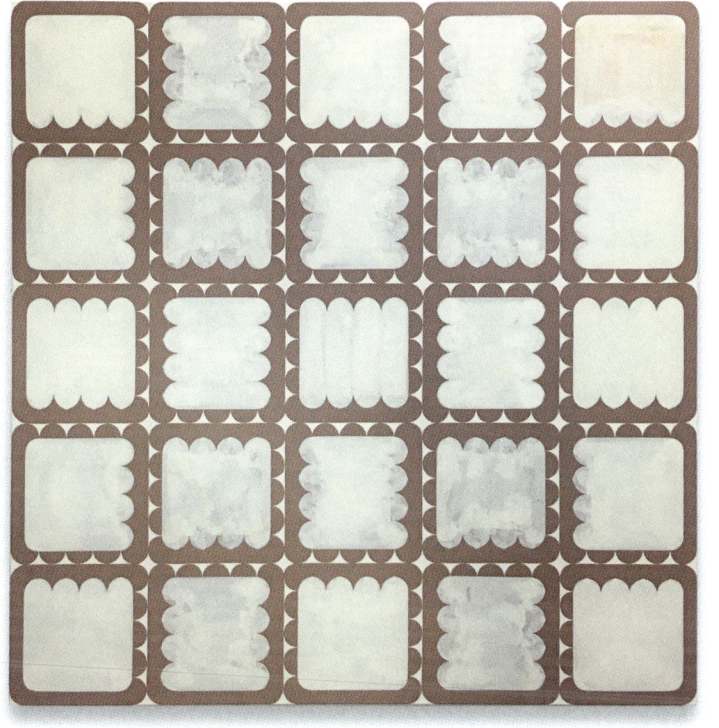
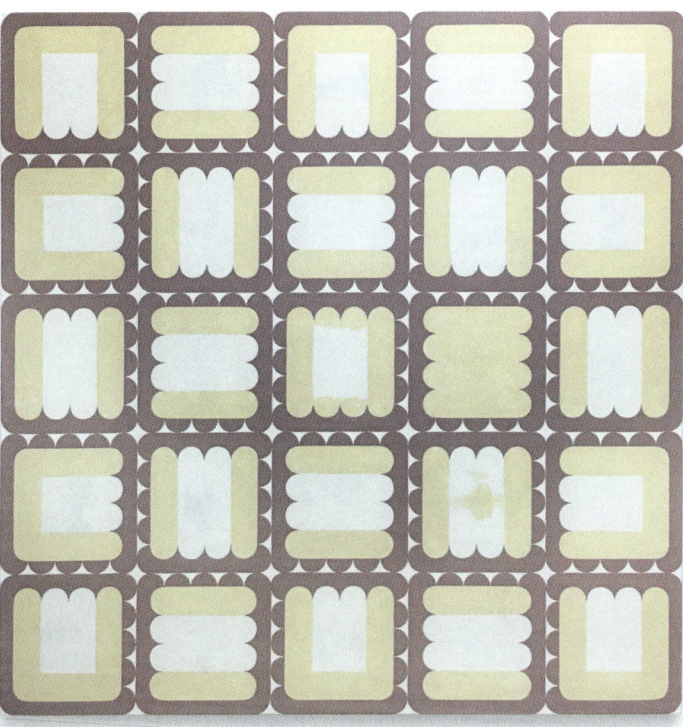

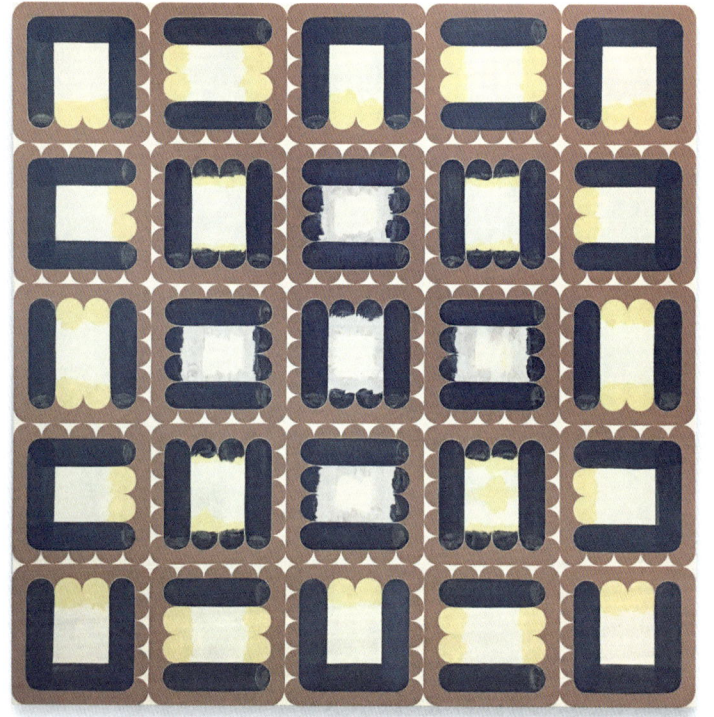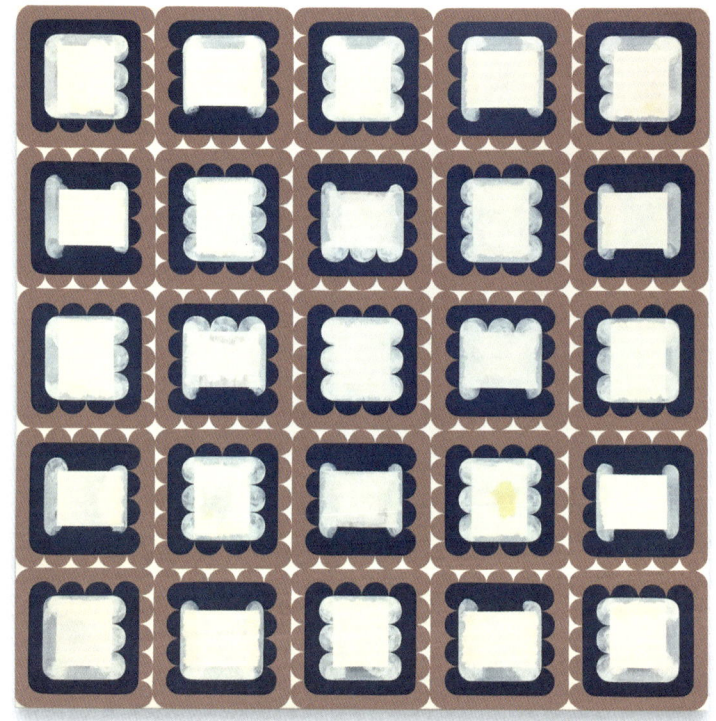

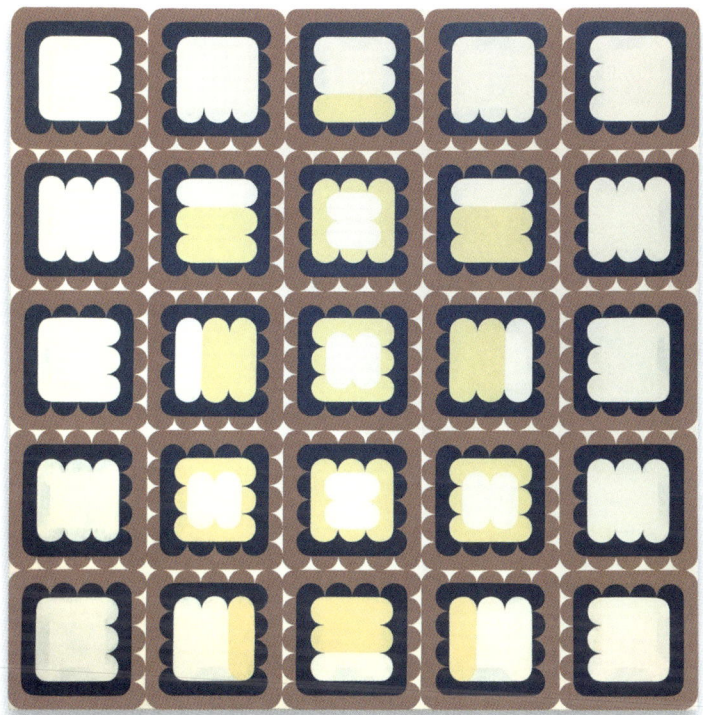

August 4, 2019

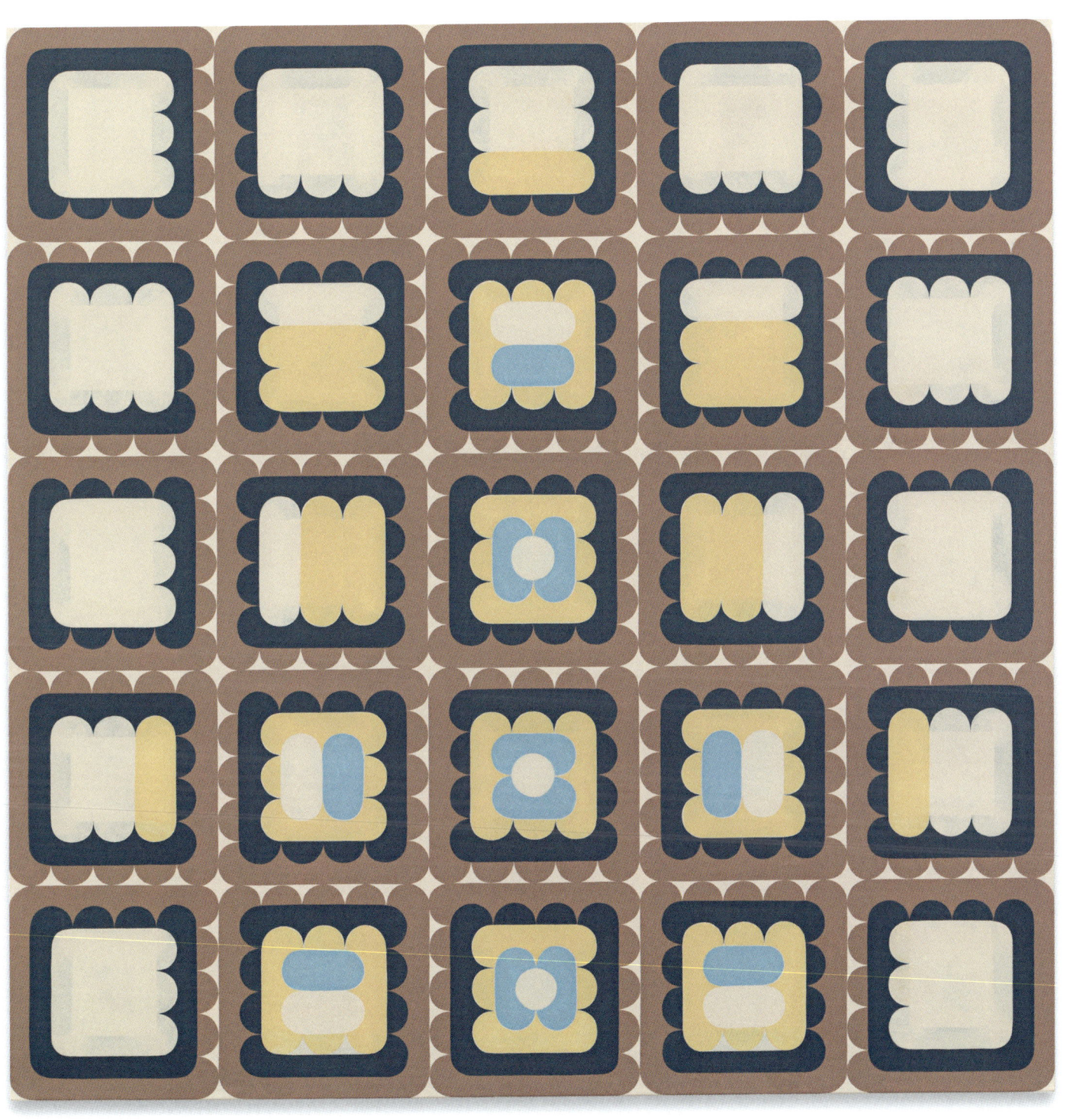

Gate, 2019, acrylic on canvas, 55×55 inches / 139.7×139.7 cm

21

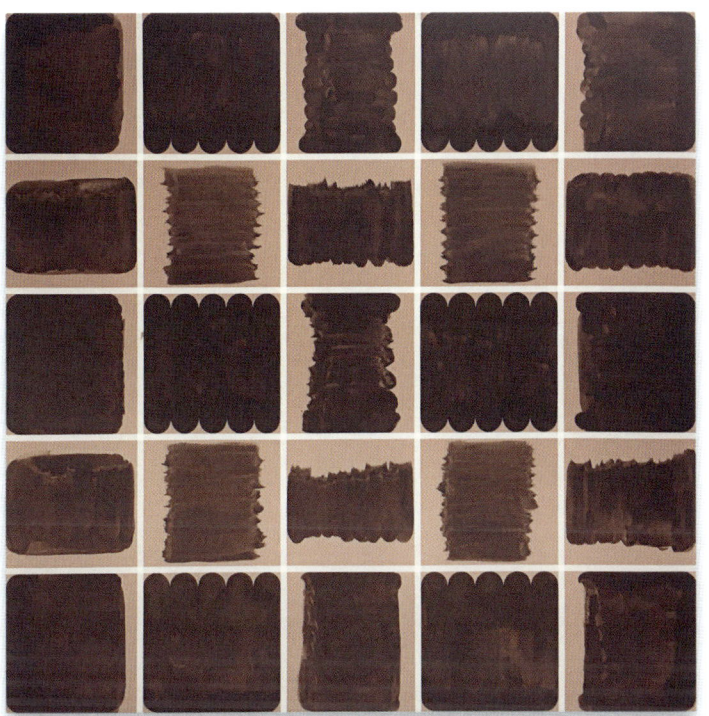

November 6, 2019

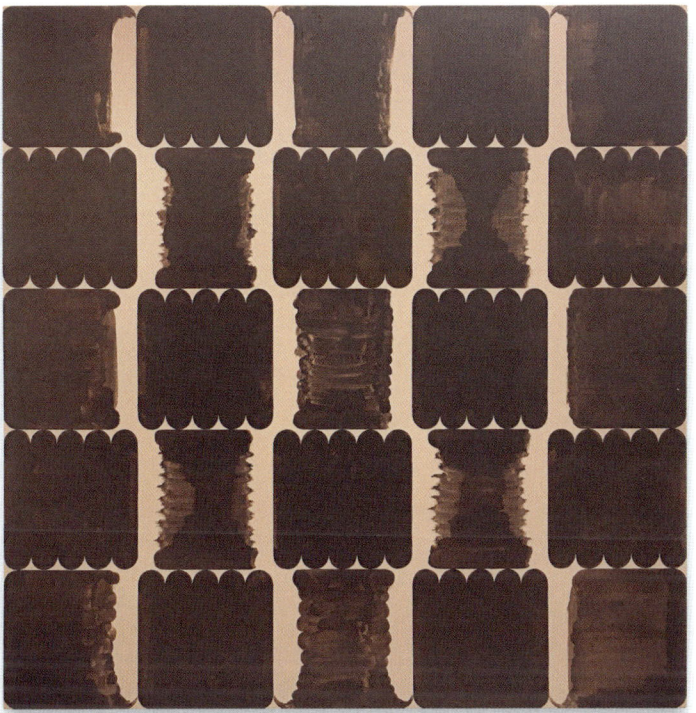

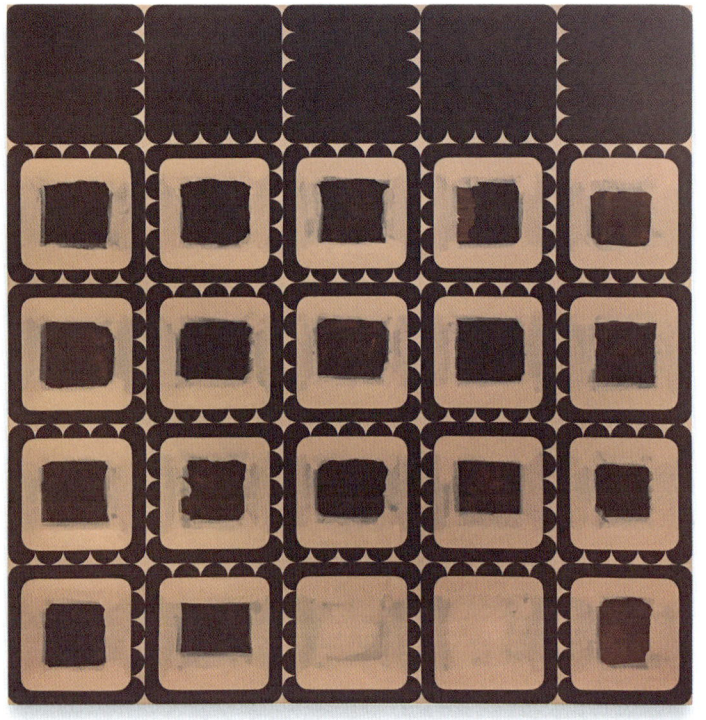 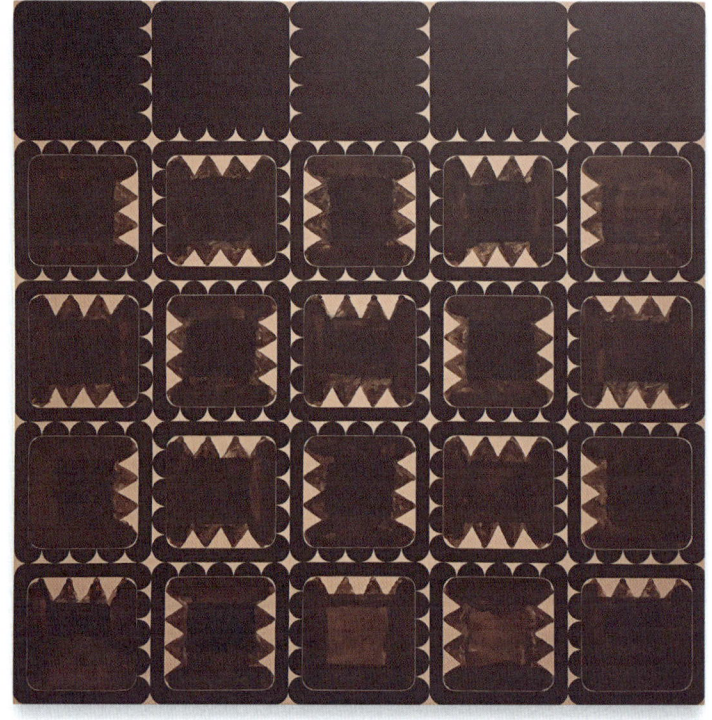

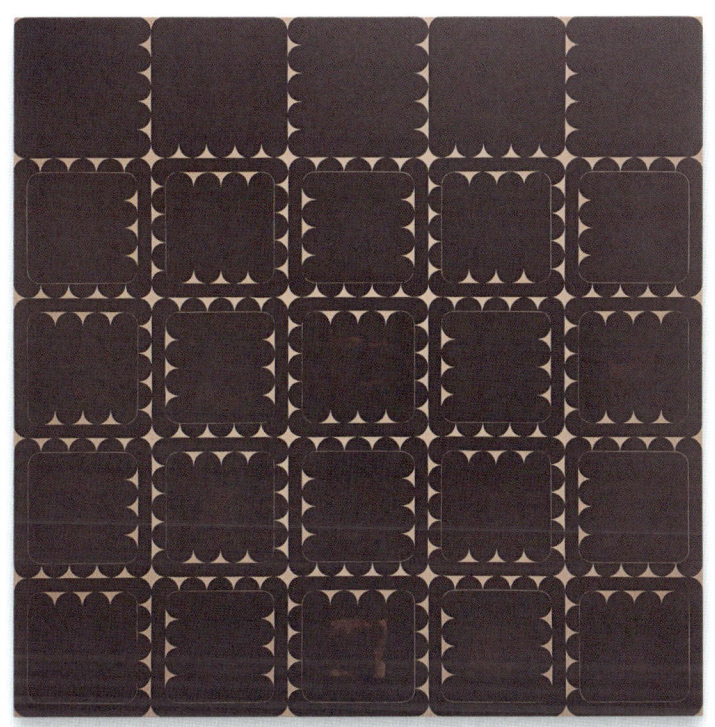
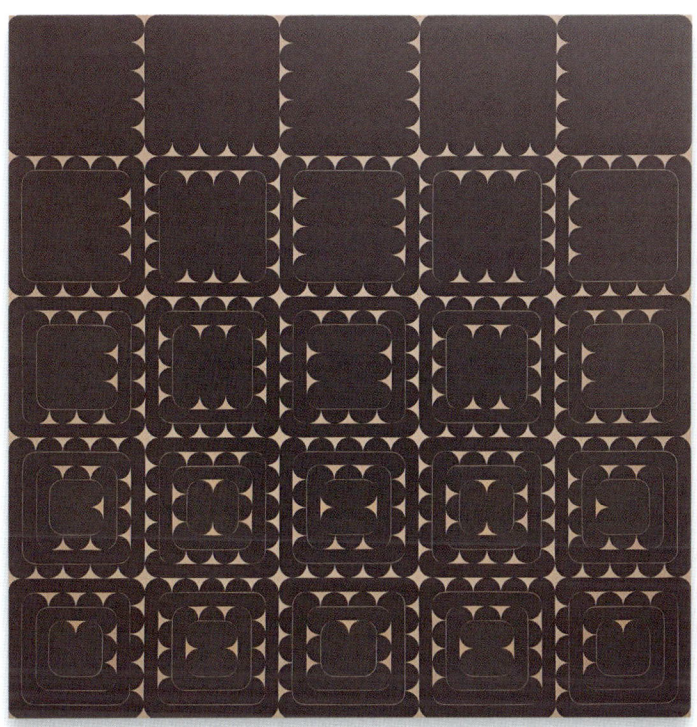

November 12, 2019

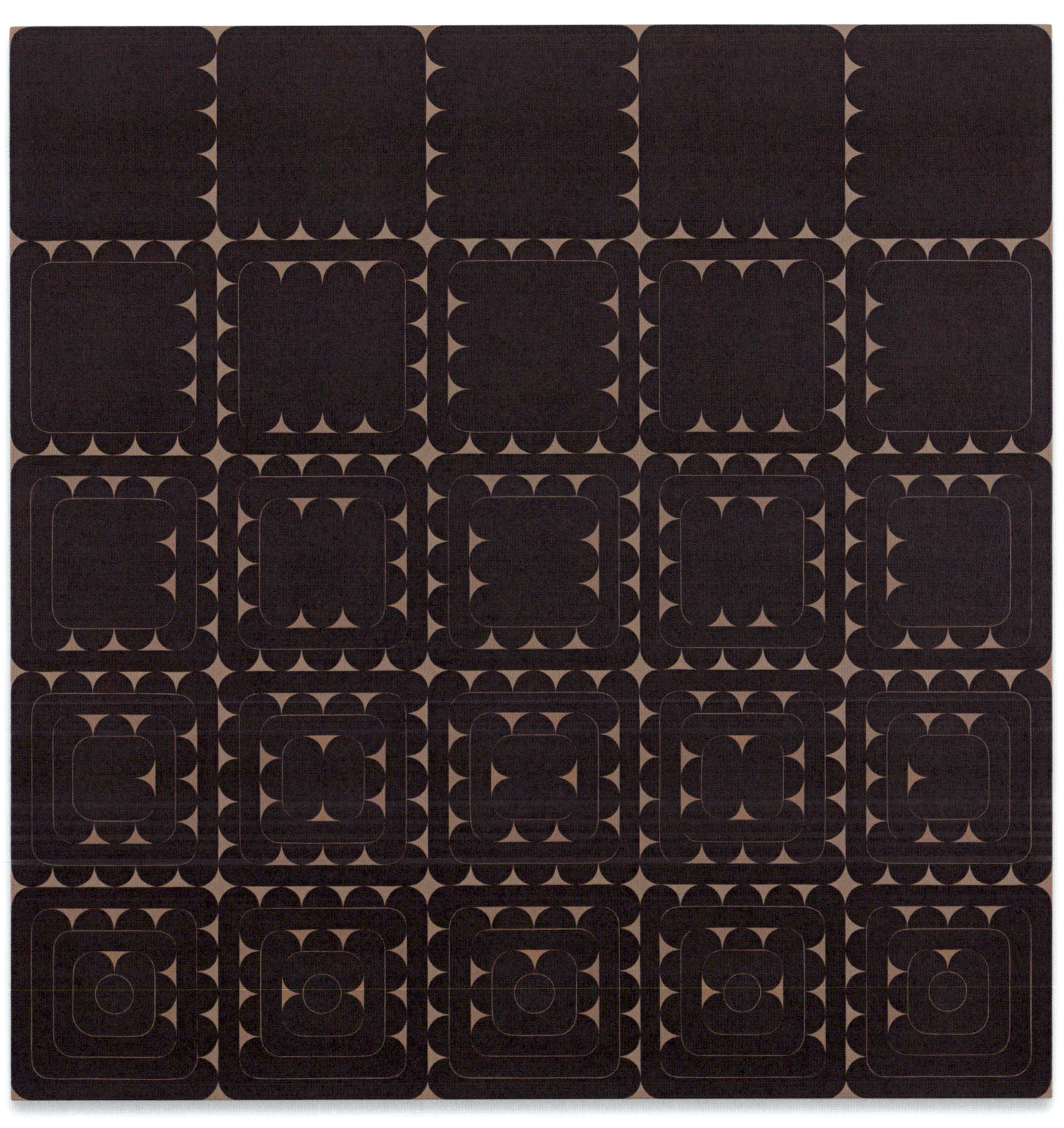

Waive, 2019, acrylic on canvas, 55×55 inches / 139.7×139.7 cm

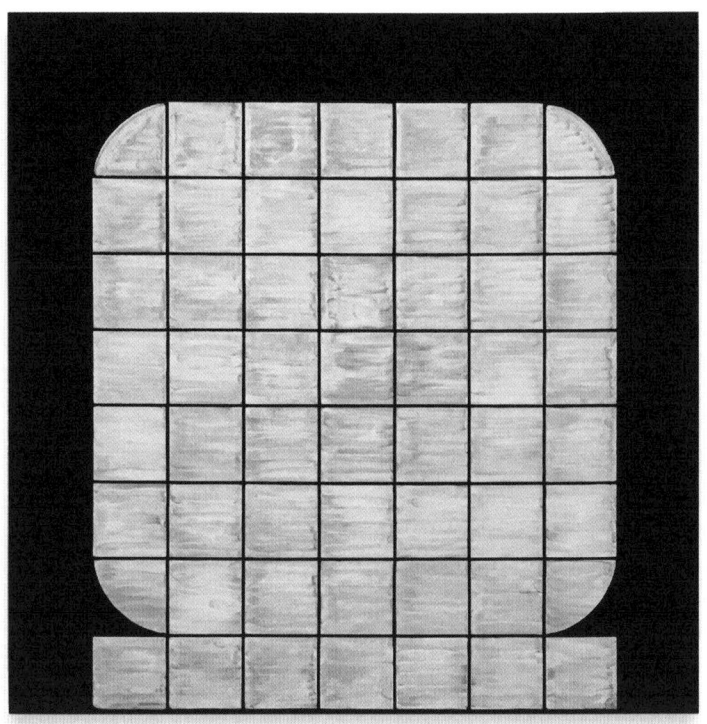

November 15, 2019

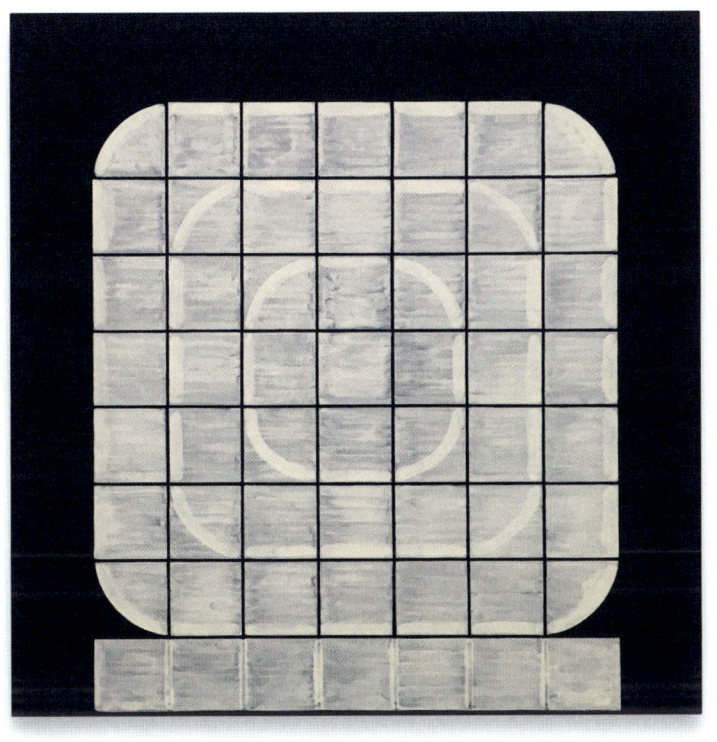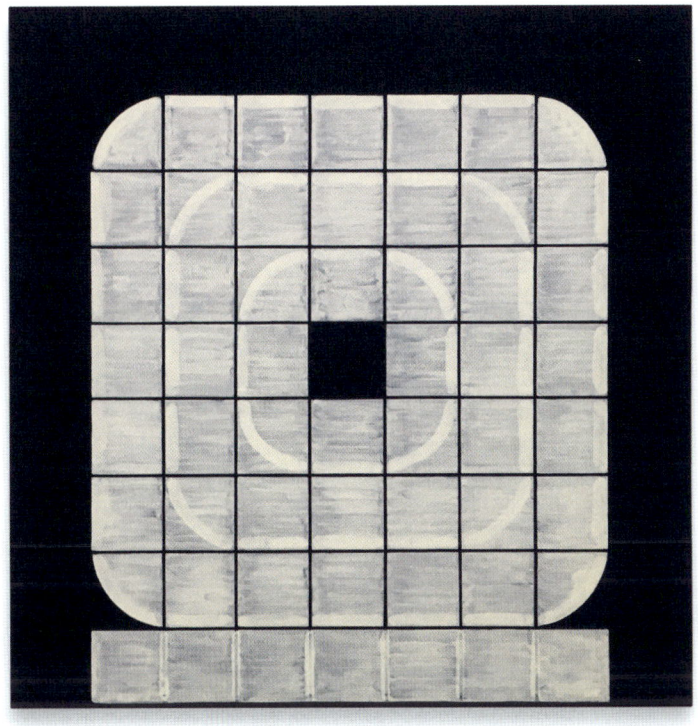

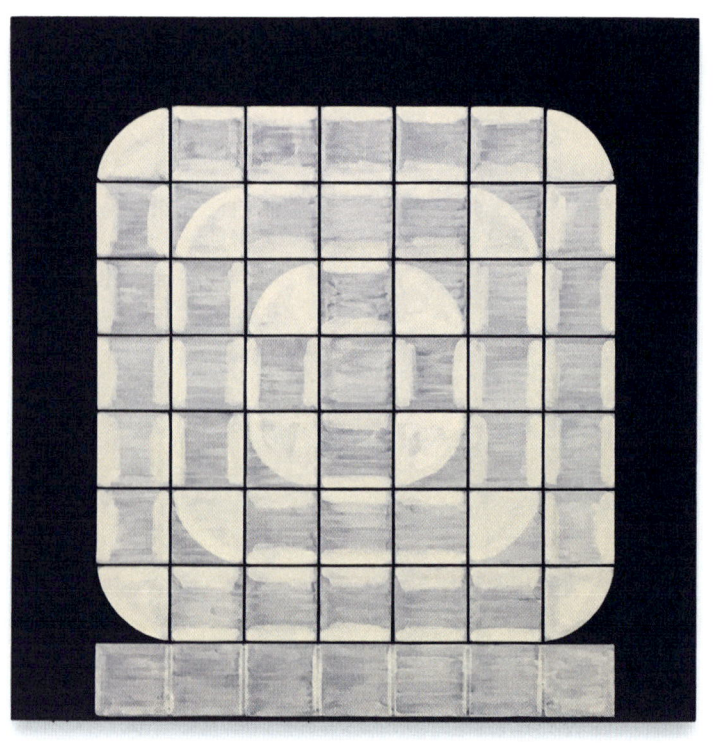 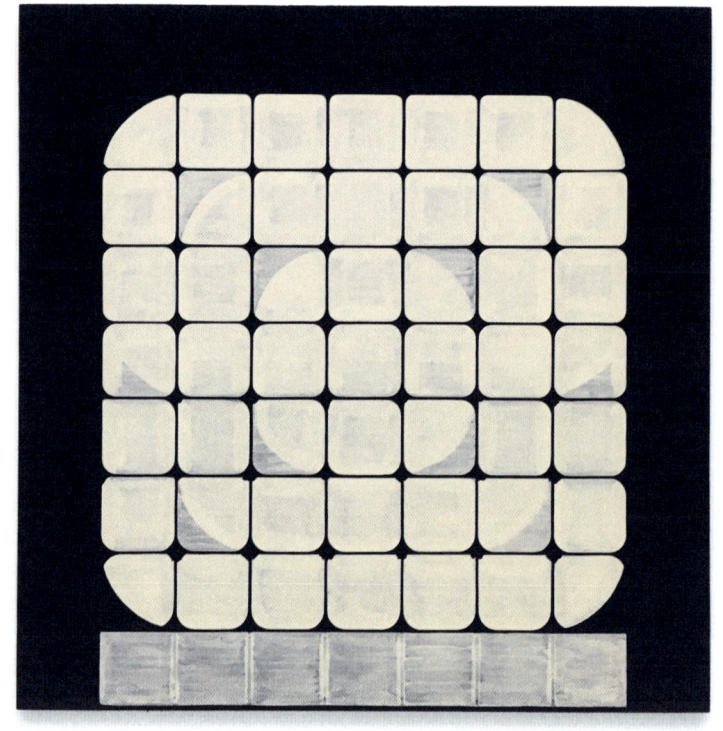

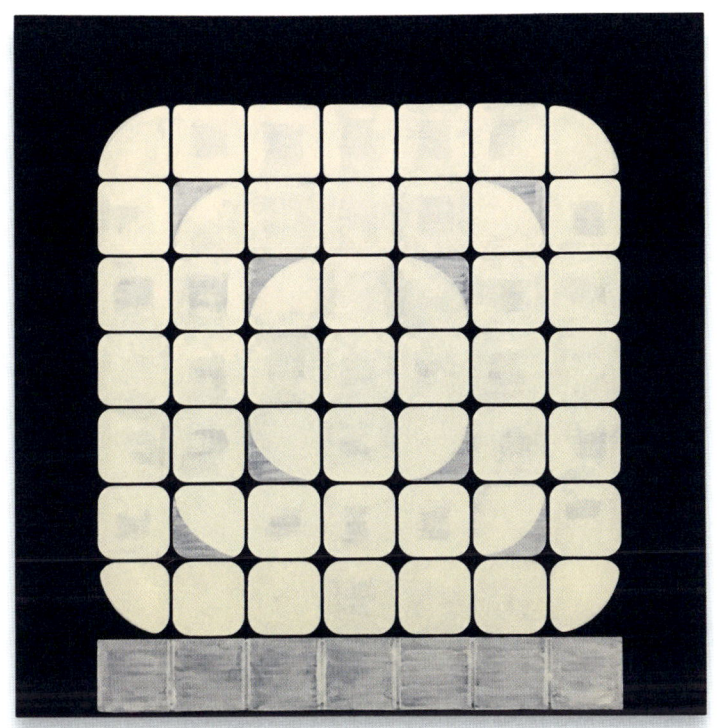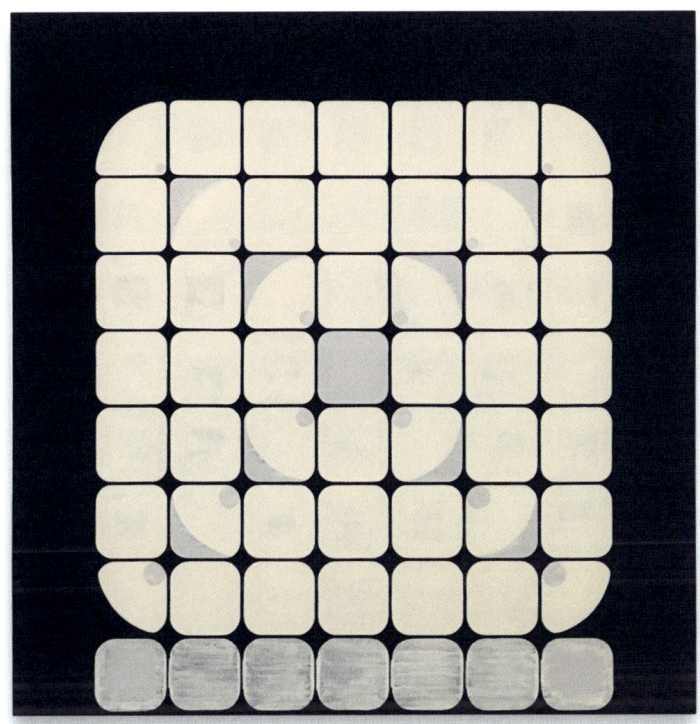

November 18, 2019

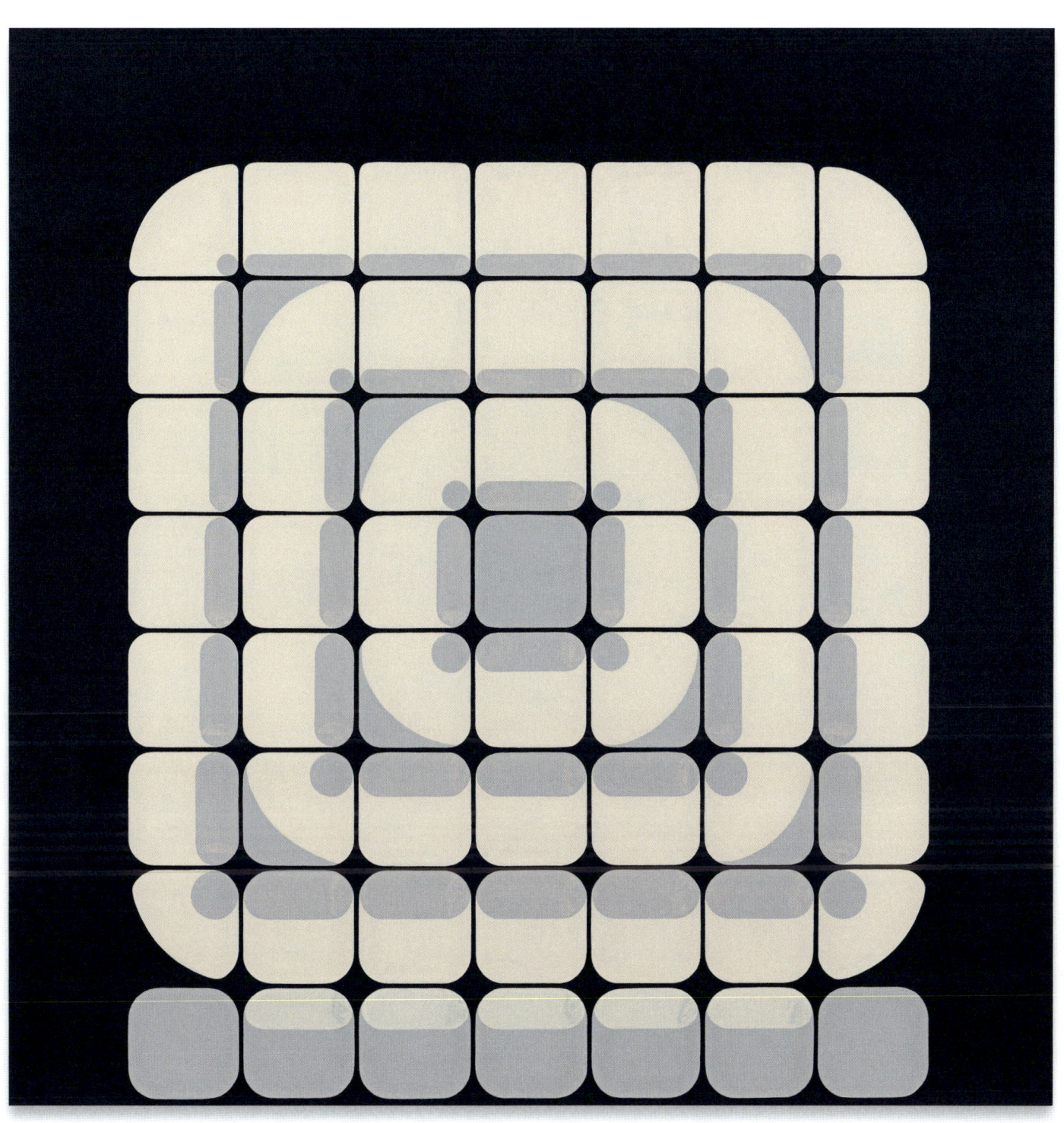

Compound, 2019, acrylic on canvas, 55×55 inches / 139.7×139.7 cm

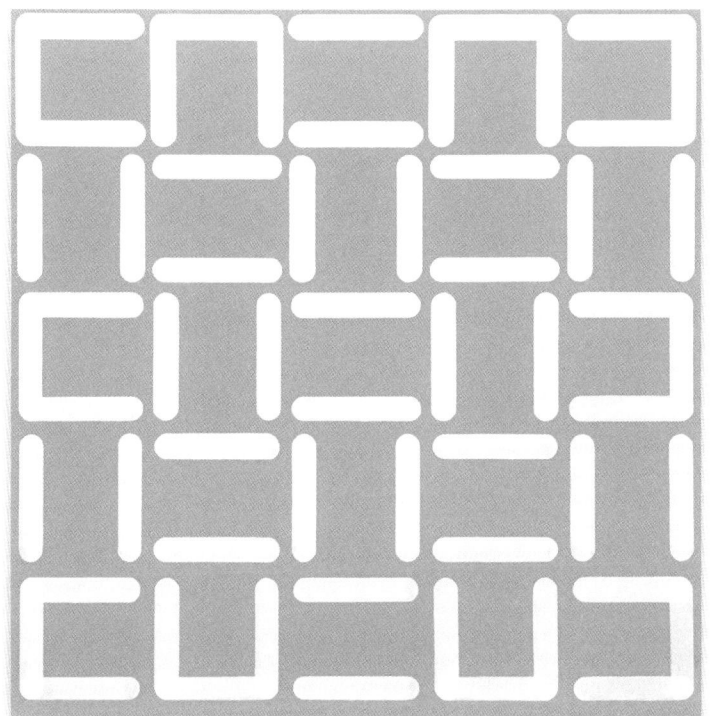

December 20, 2019

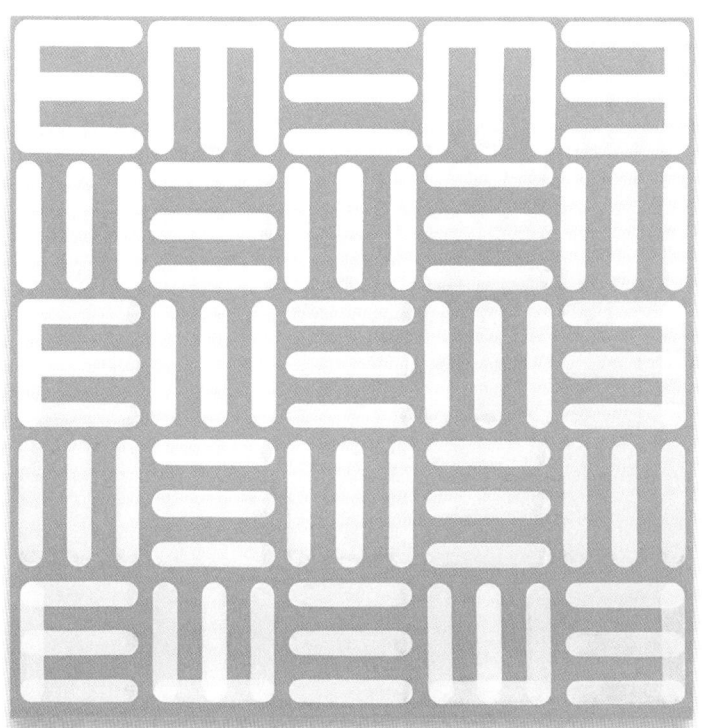

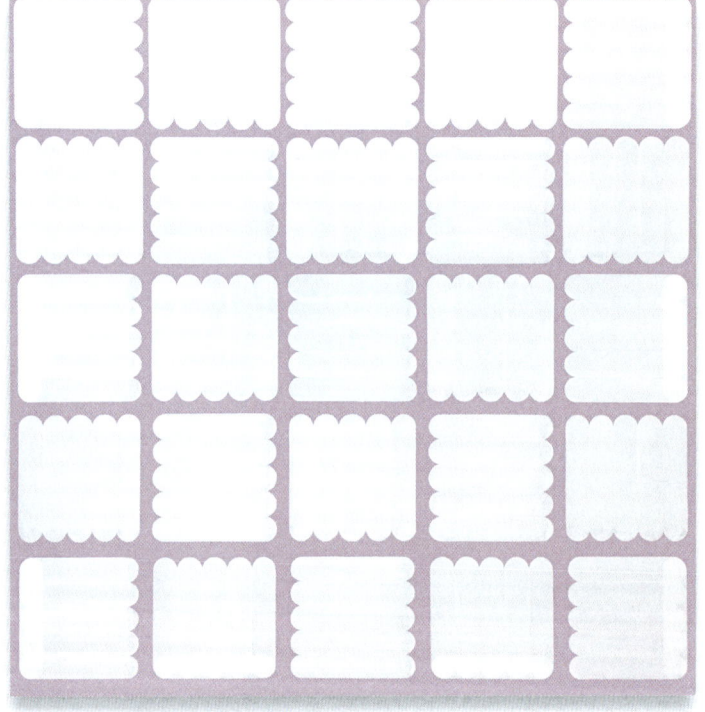
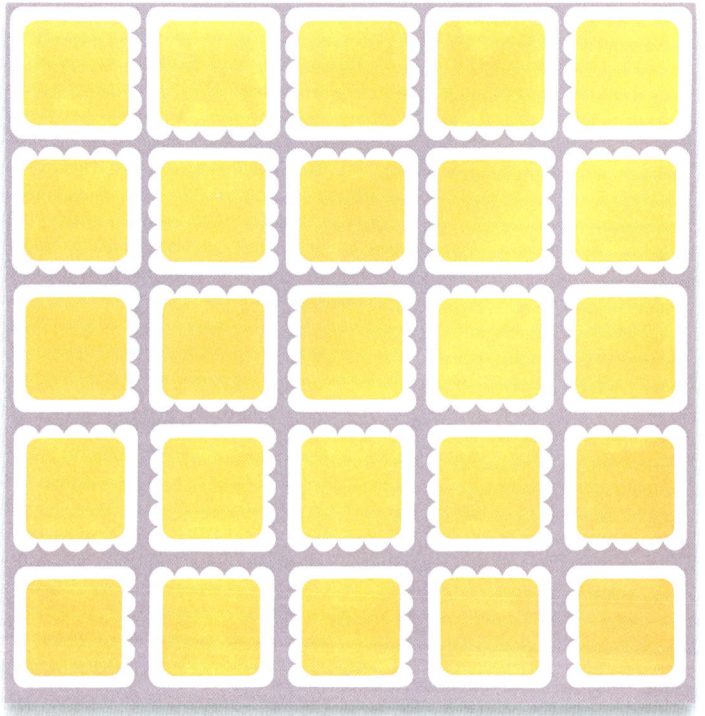

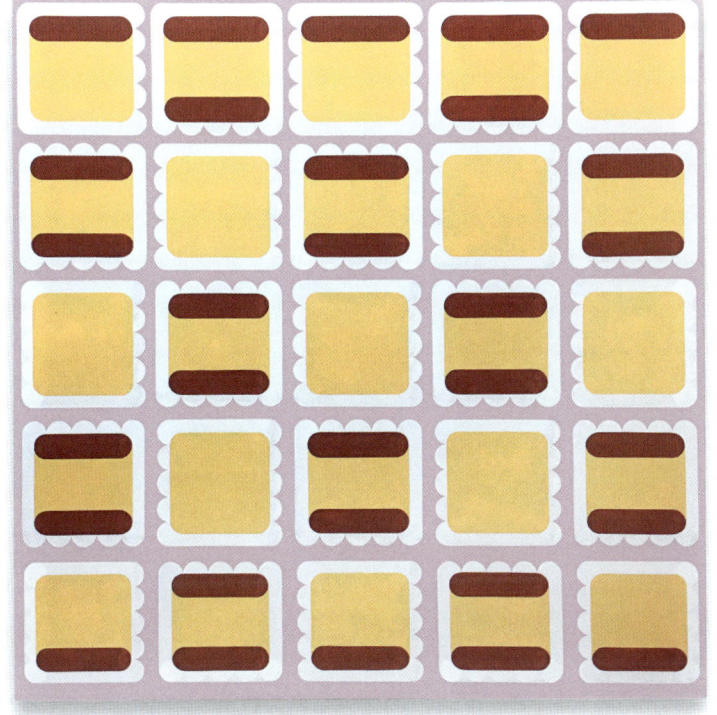
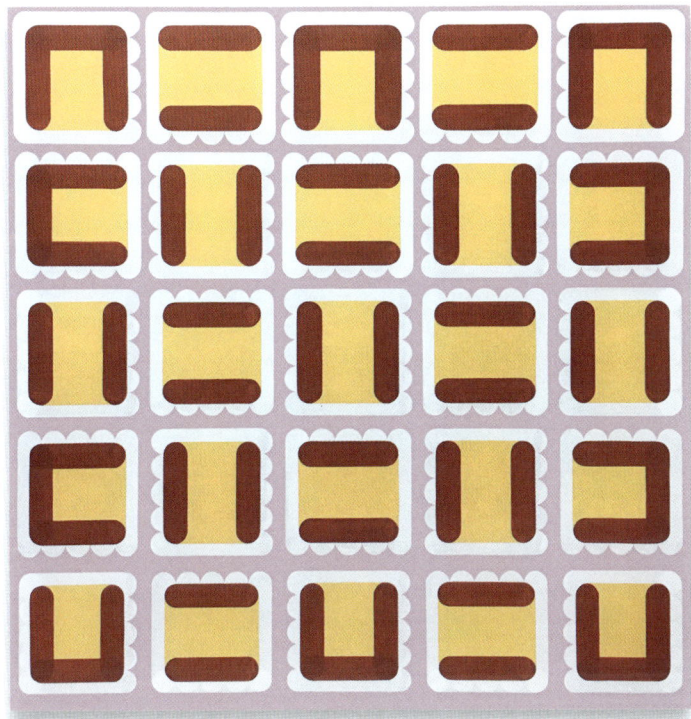

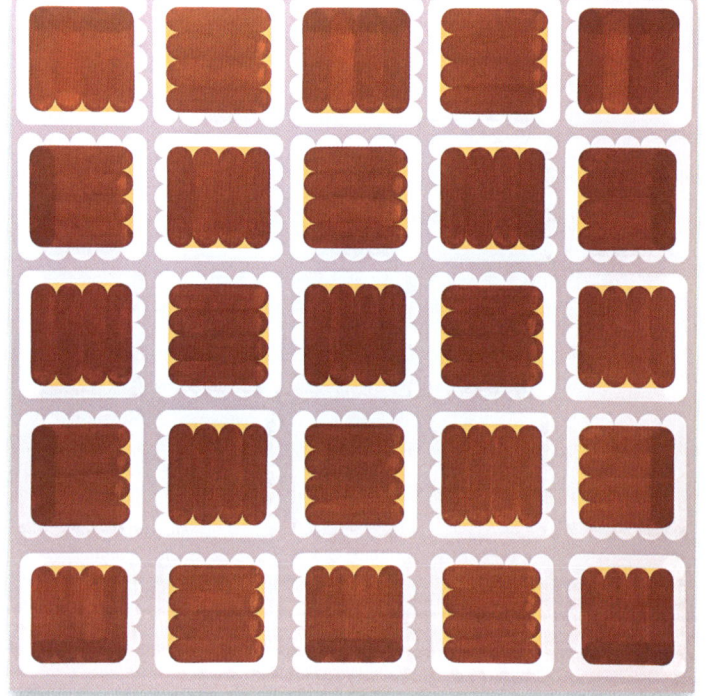
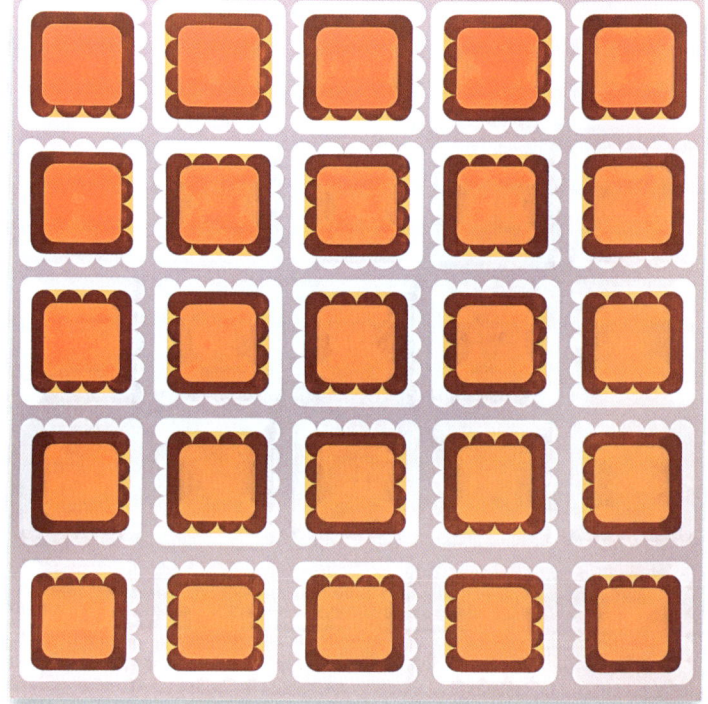

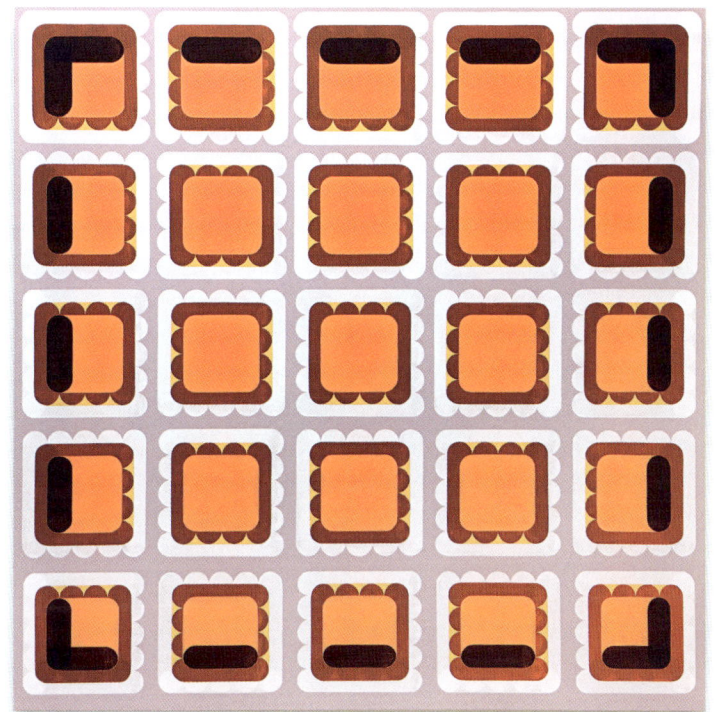

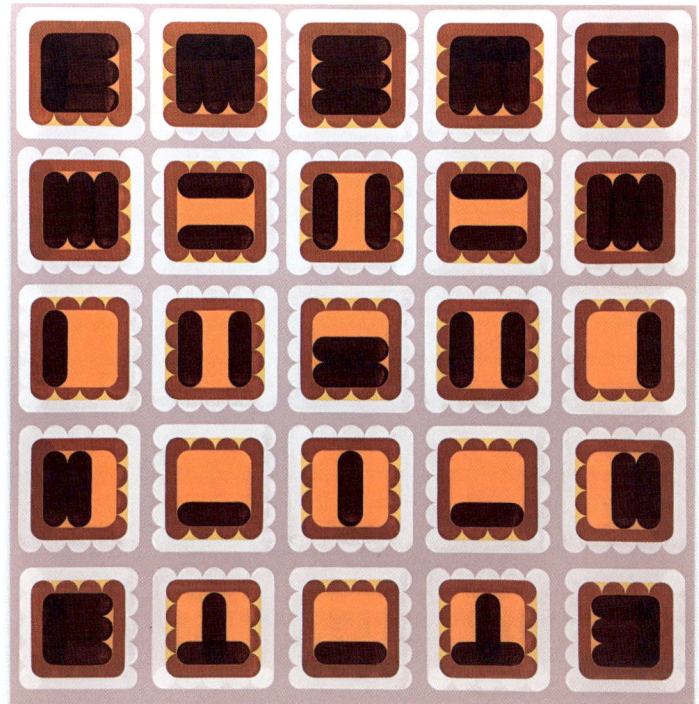

January 3, 2020

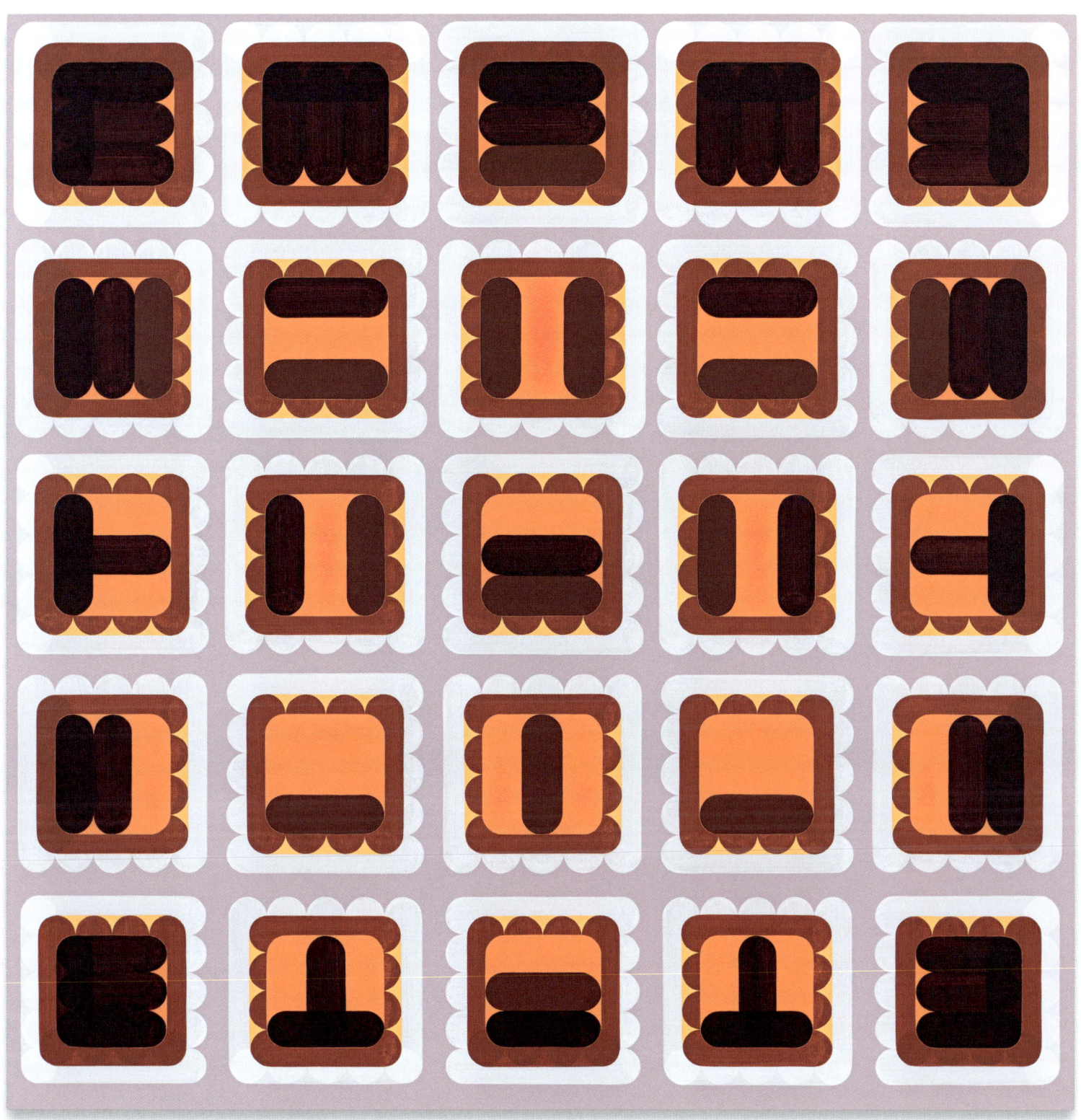

Score, 2020, acrylic on canvas, 70×70 inches / 177.8×177.8 cm

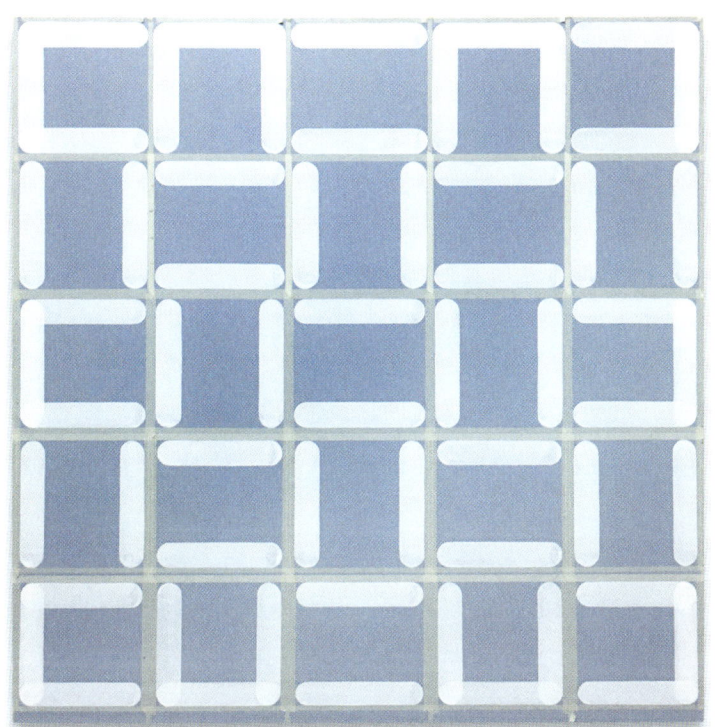
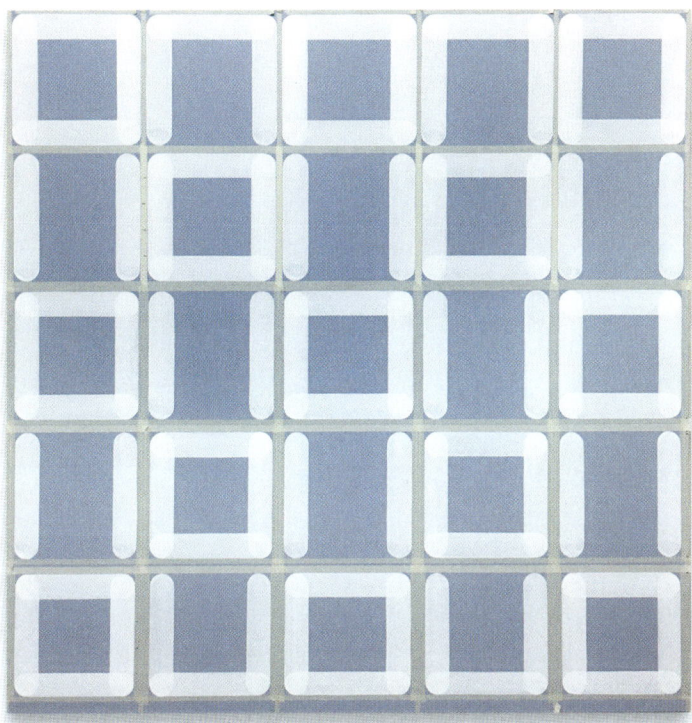

February 9, 2020

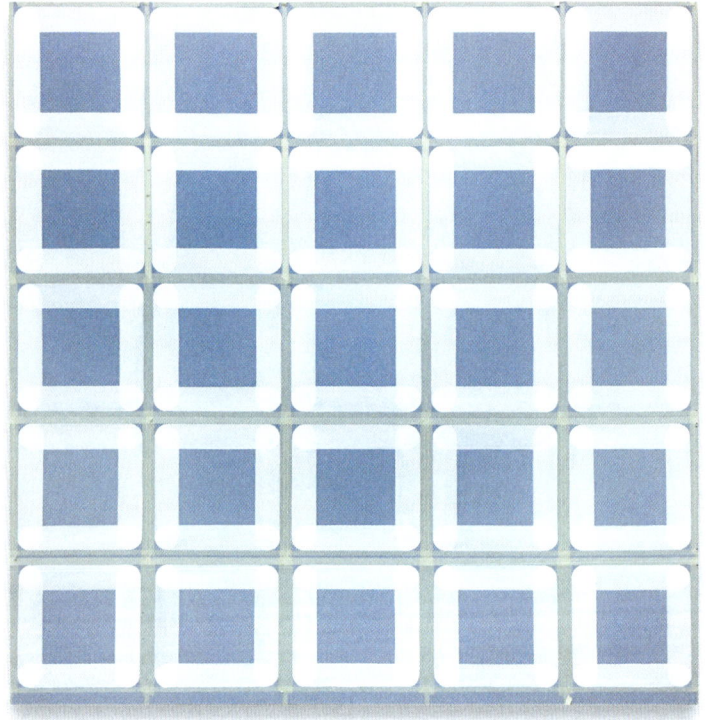 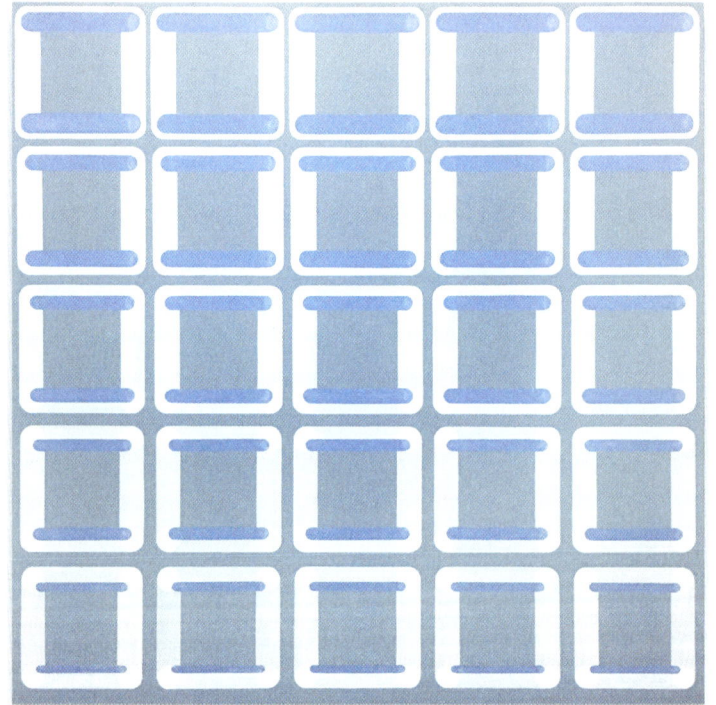

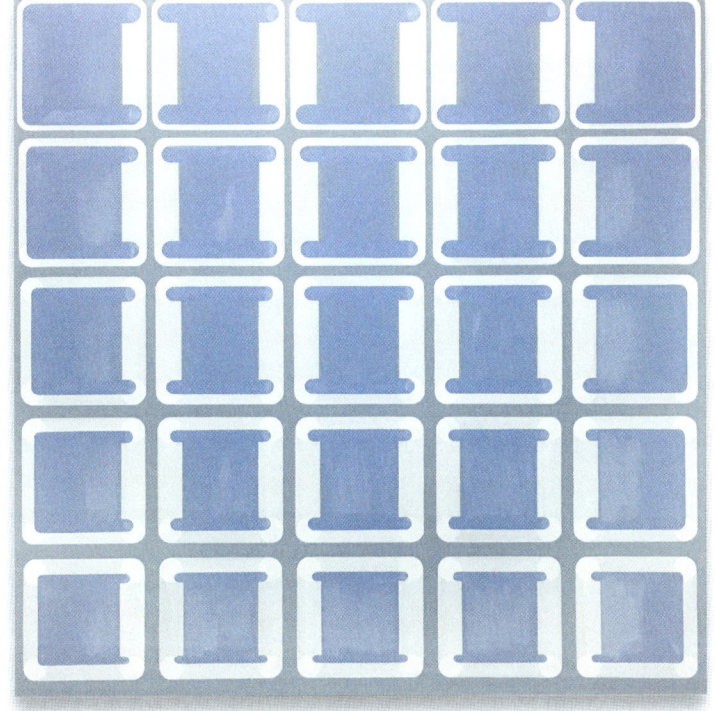

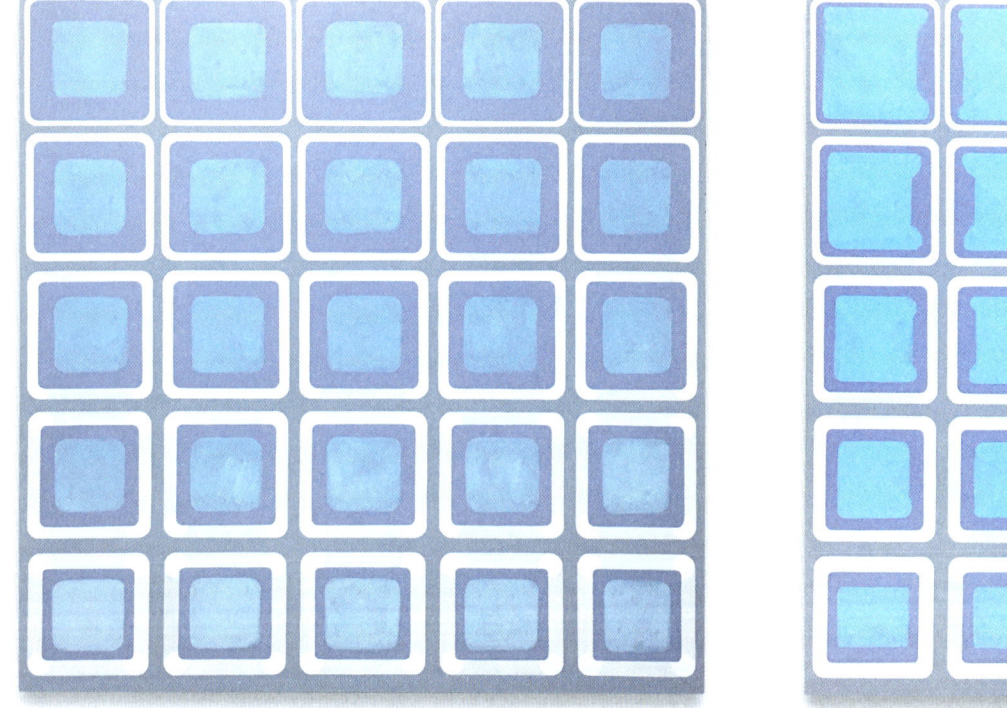
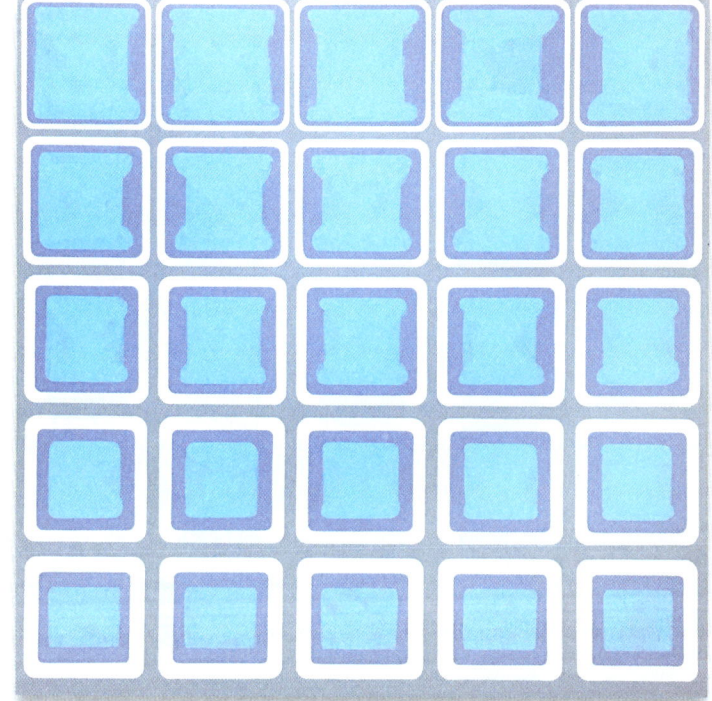

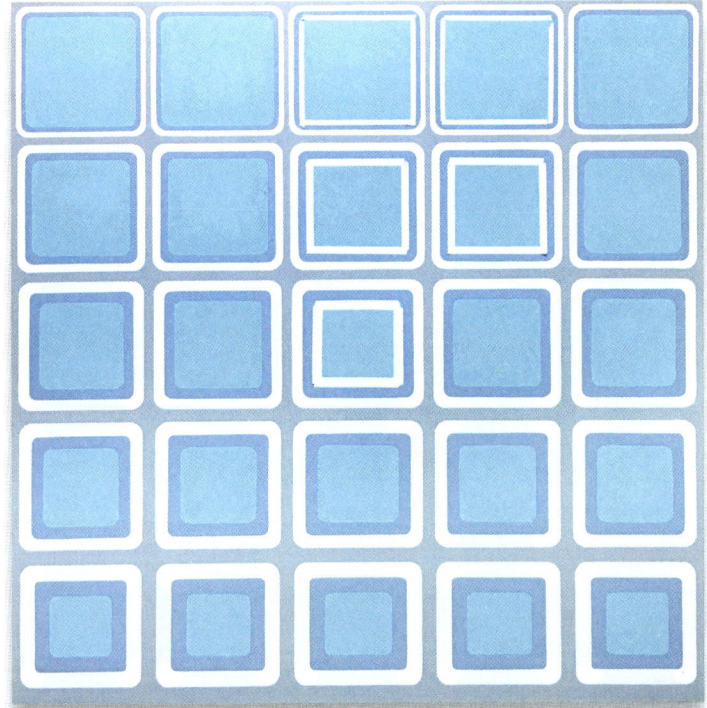

February 24, 2020

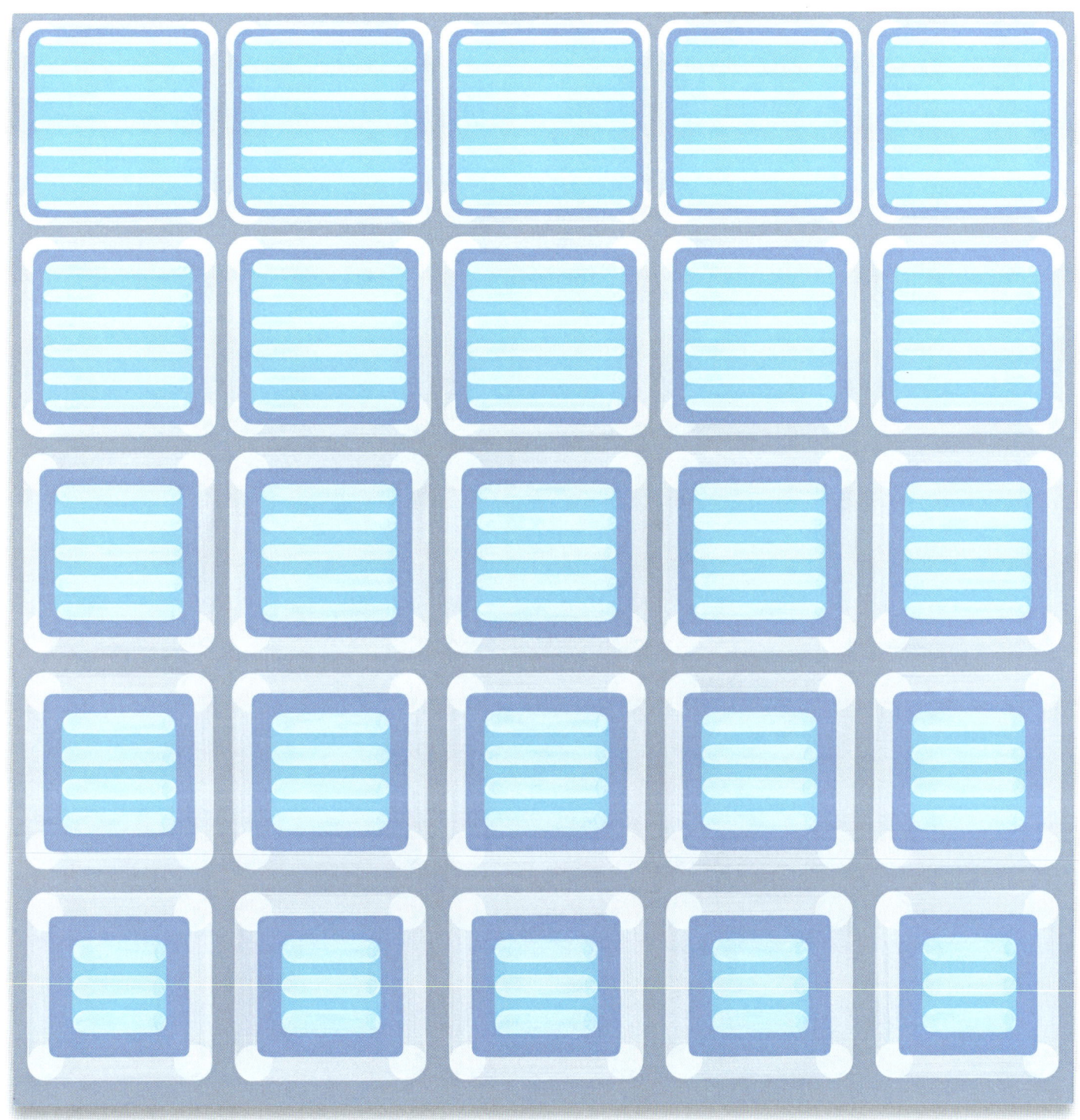

Wake, 2020, acrylic on canvas, 55×55 inches / 139.7×139.7 cm

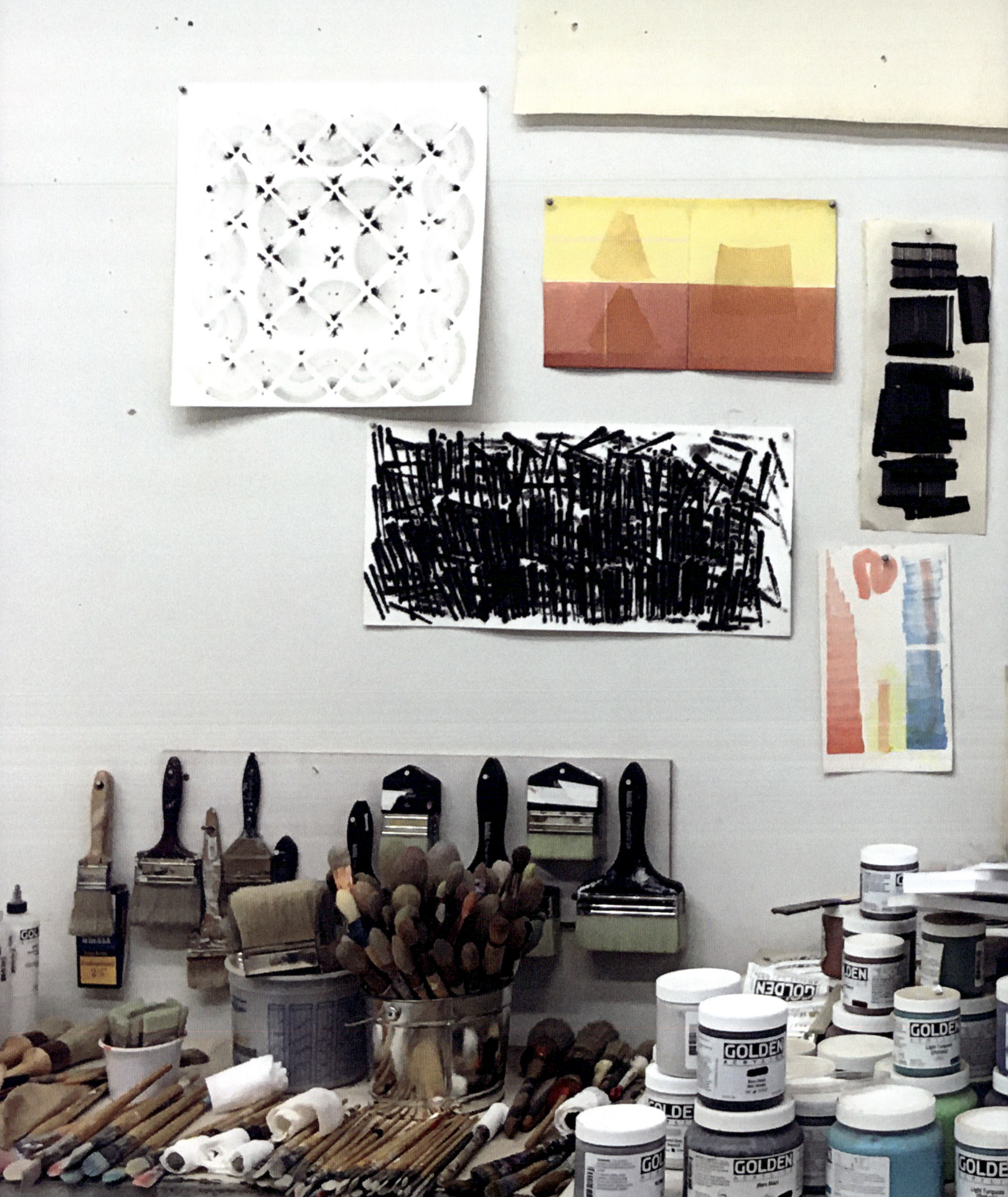

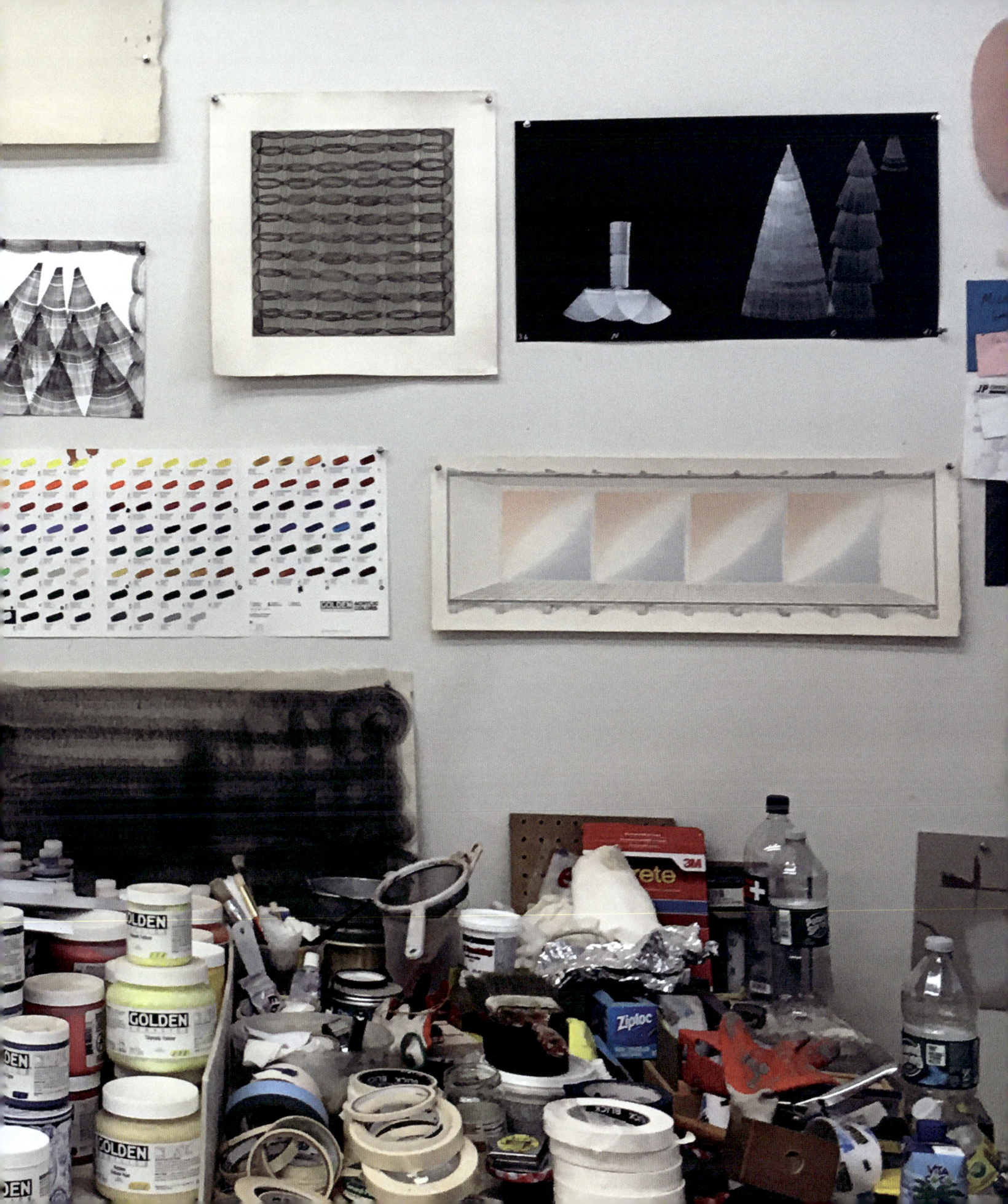

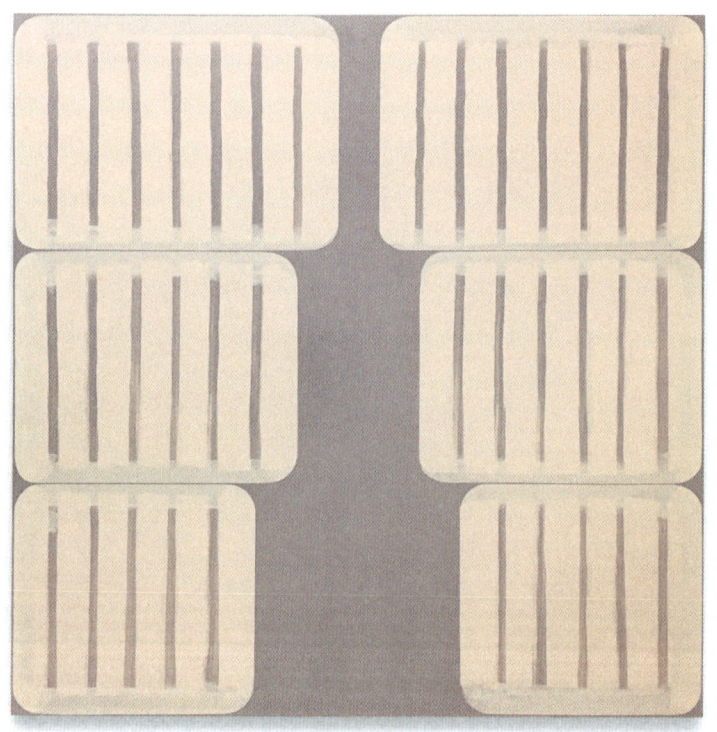

March 24, 2020

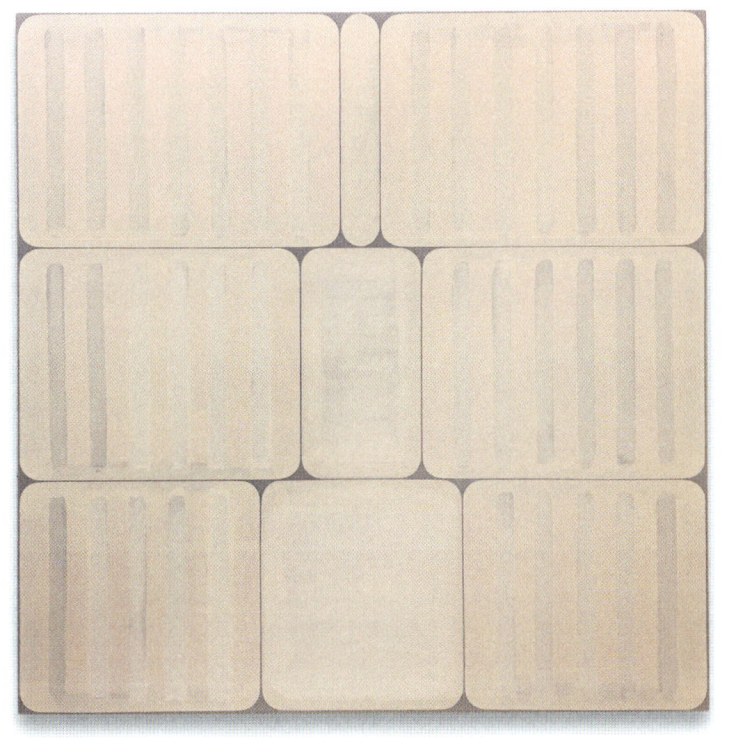 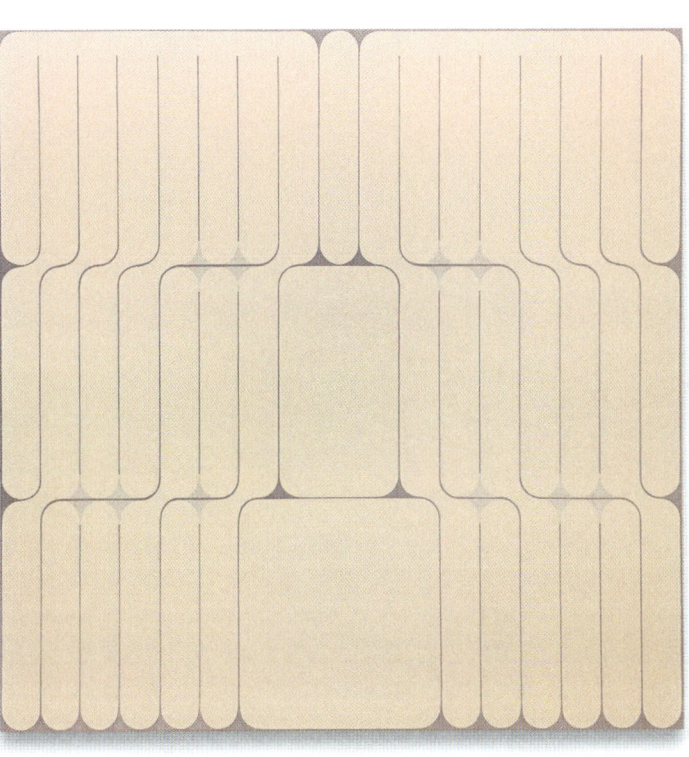

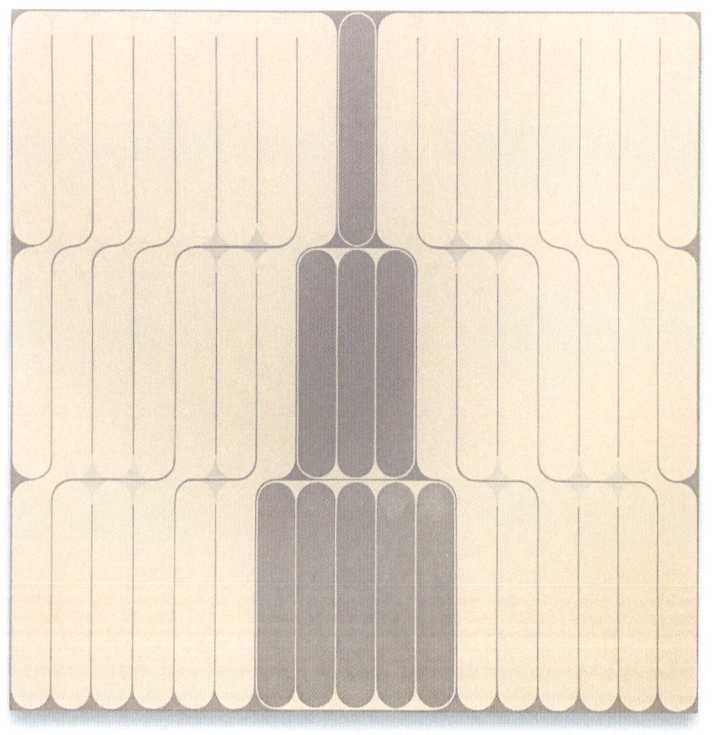
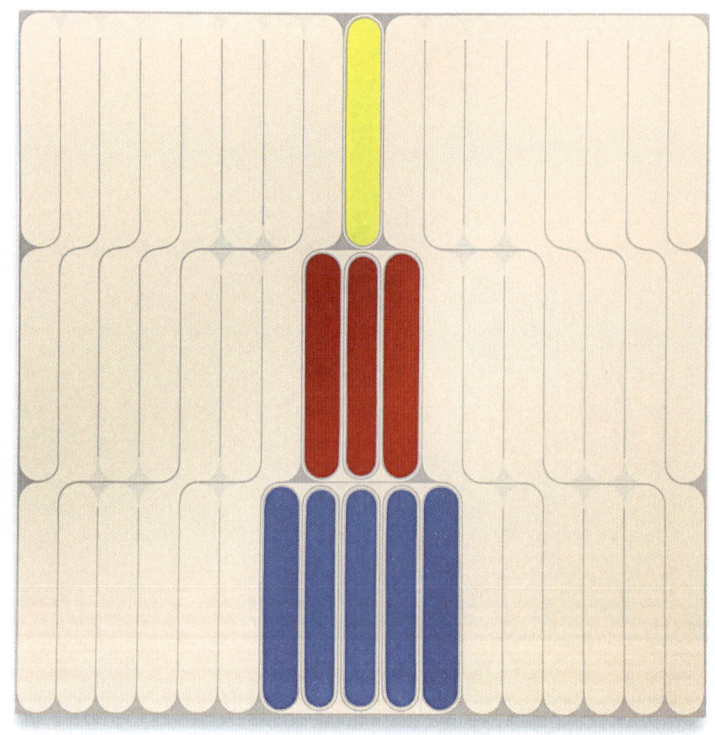

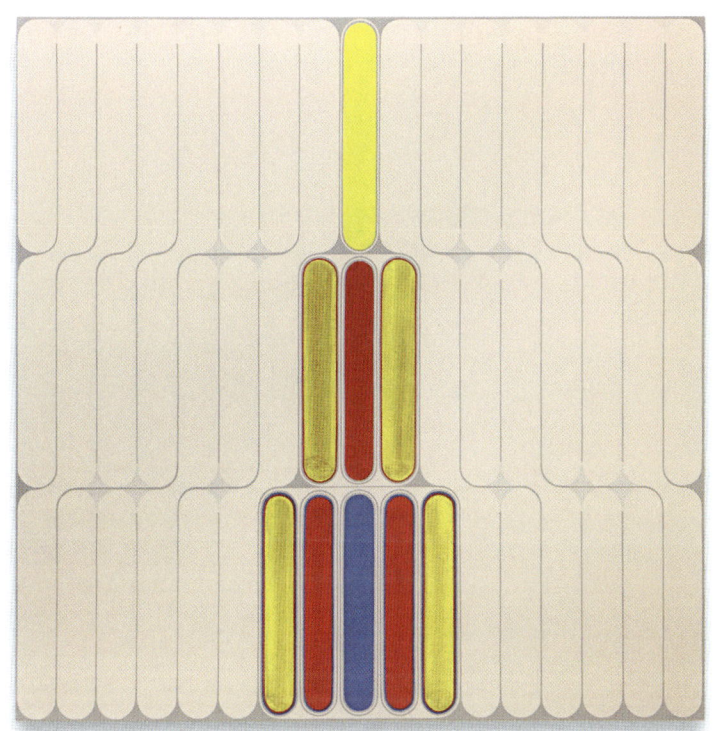 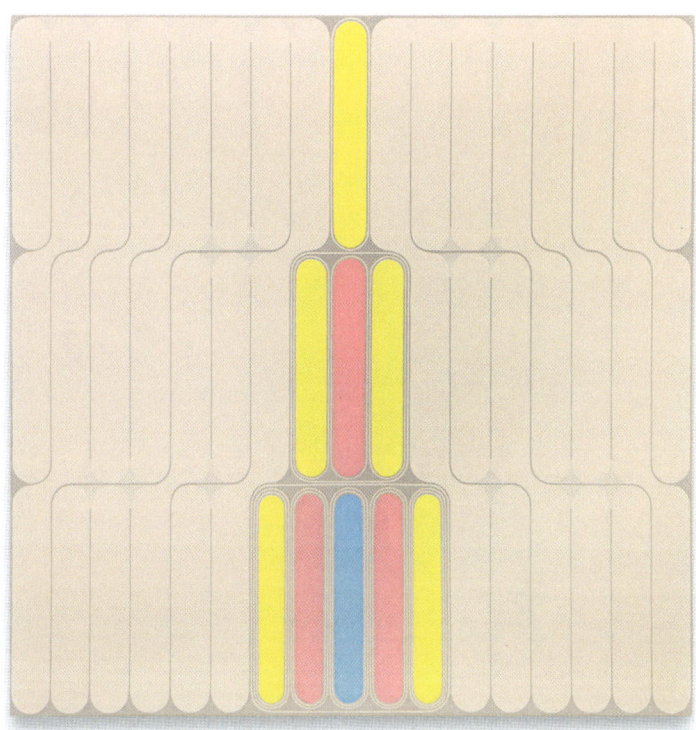

April 11, 2020

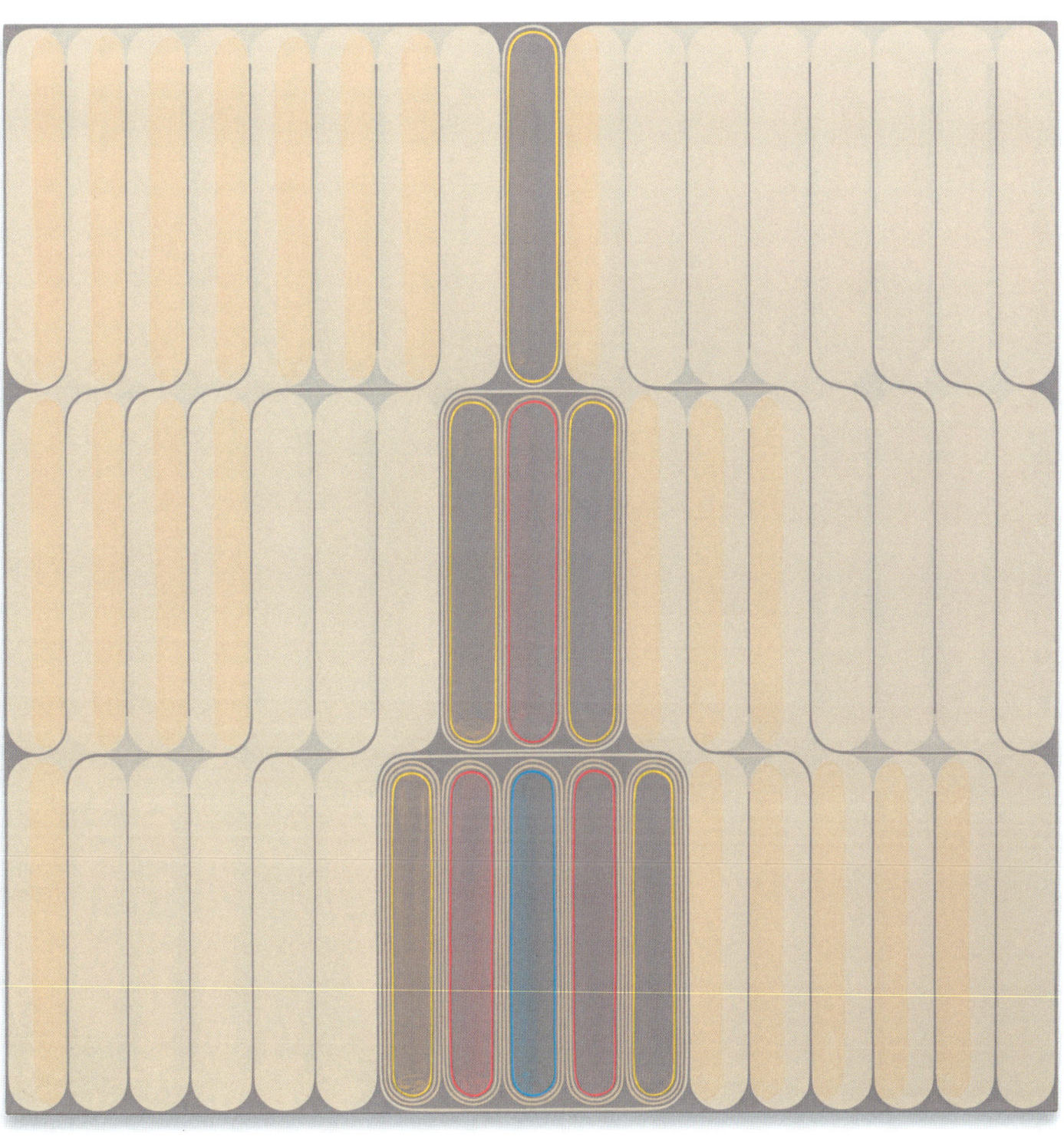

Prime, 2020, acrylic on canvas, 55×55 inches / 139.7×139.7 cm

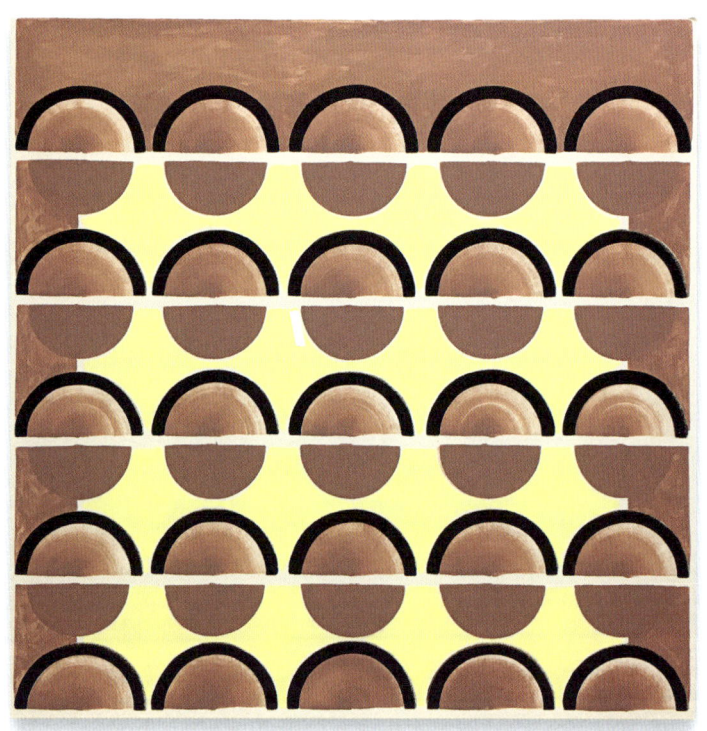
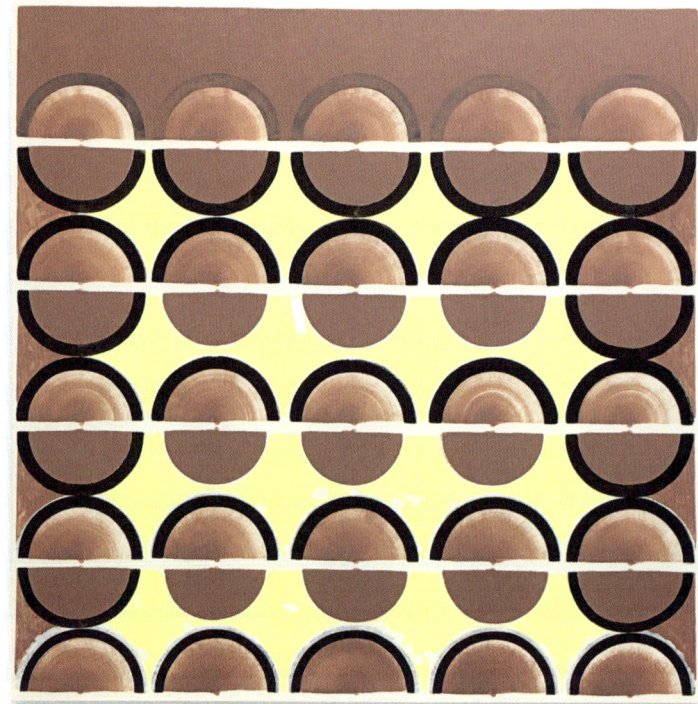

February 24, 2020

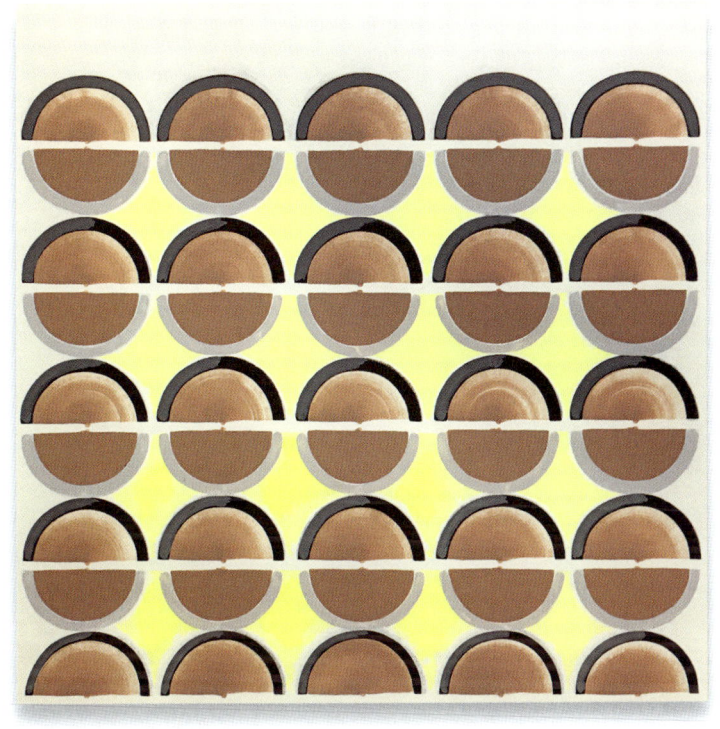

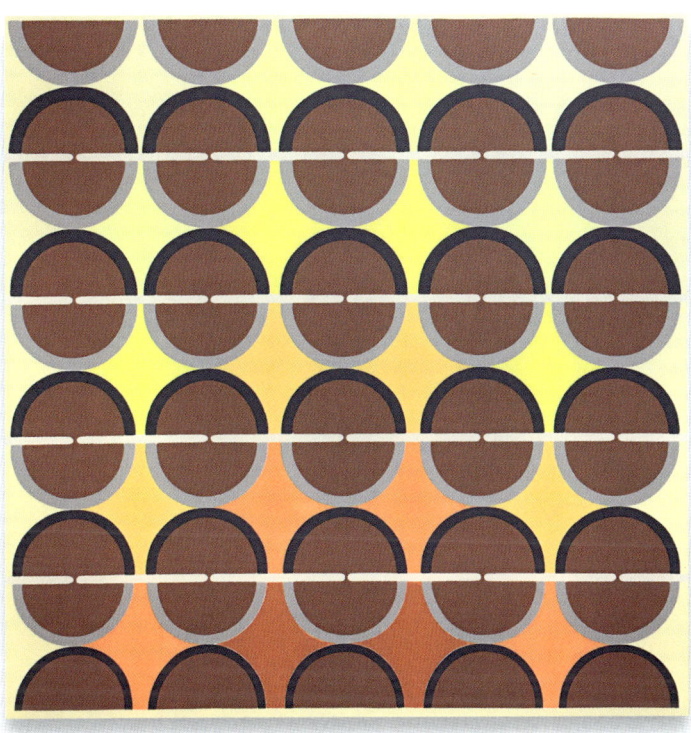

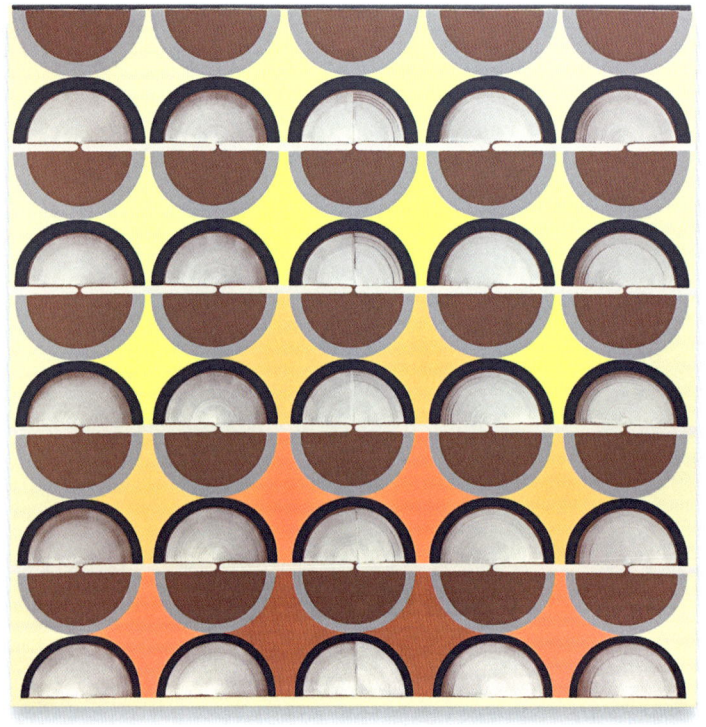 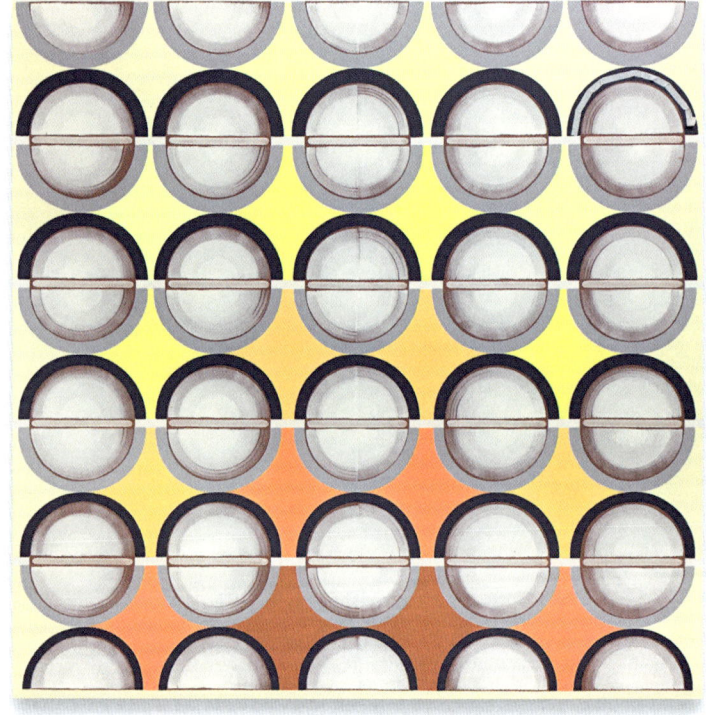

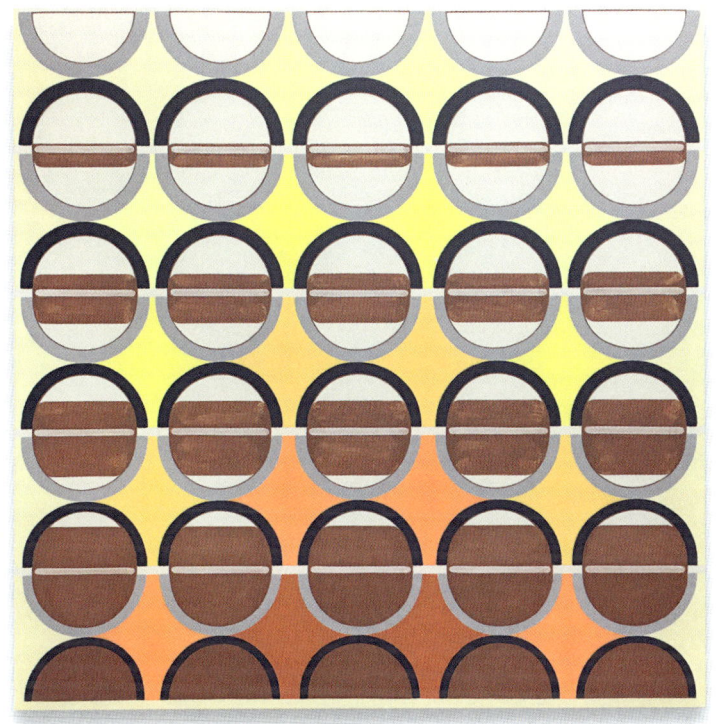 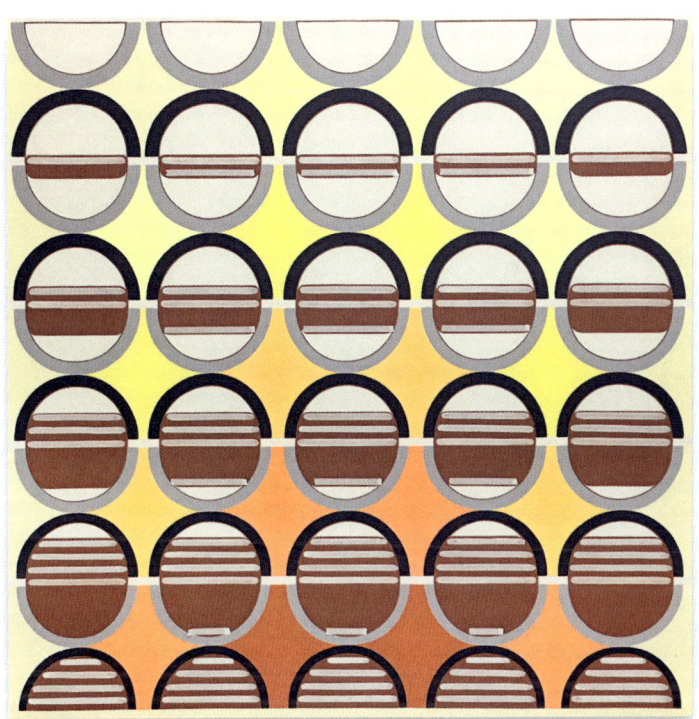

March 18, 2020

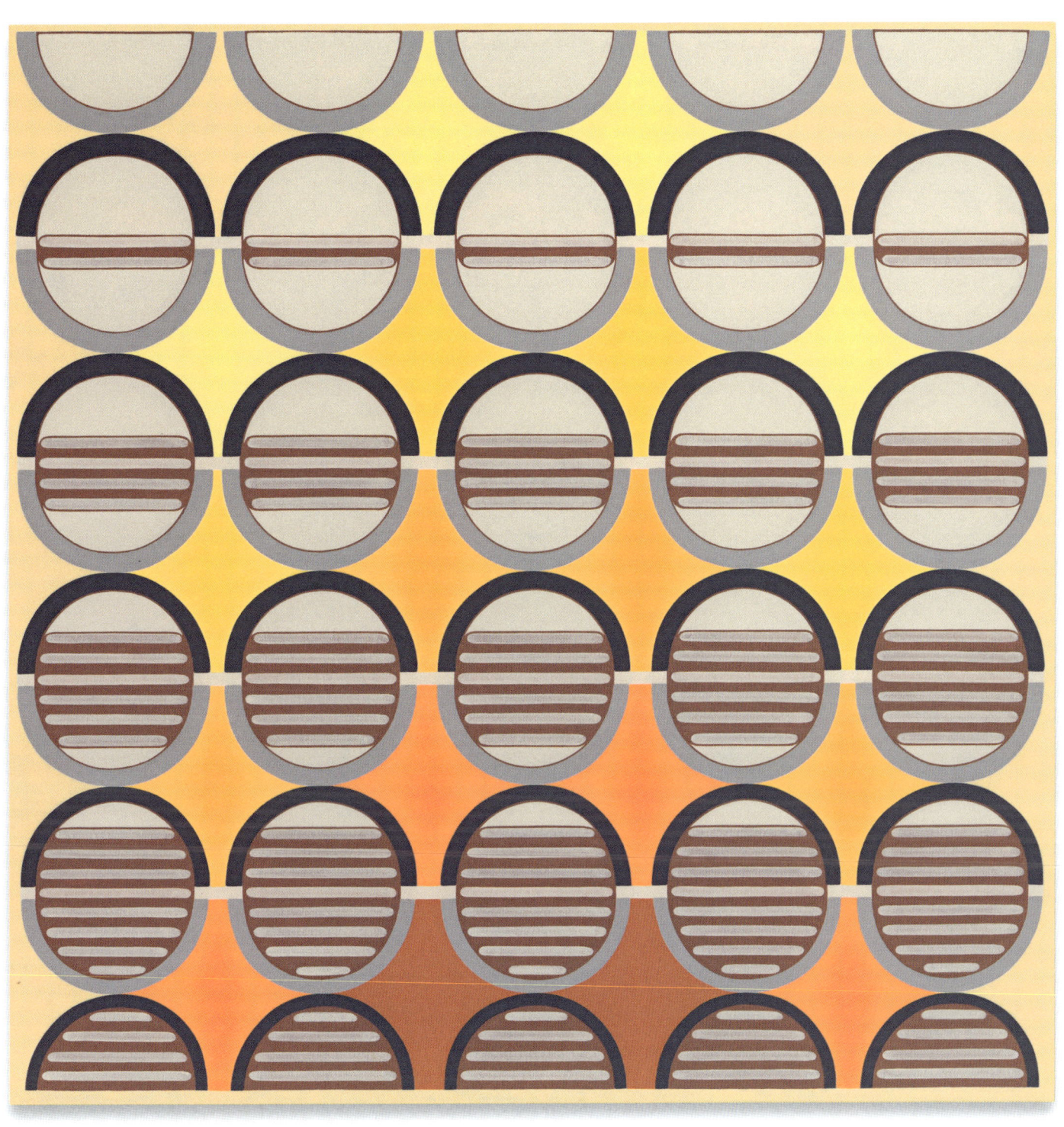

Eclipse, 2020, acrylic on canvas, 55×55 inches / 139.7×139.7 cm

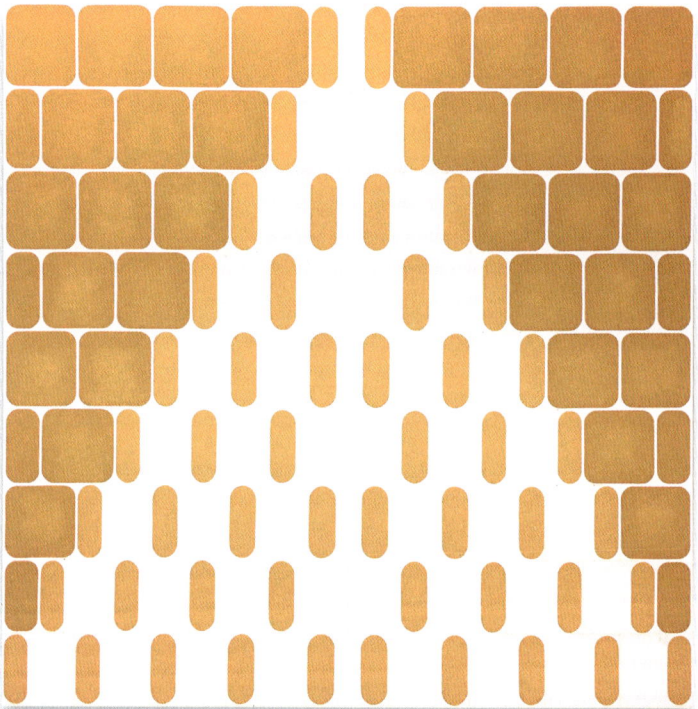

April 5, 2021

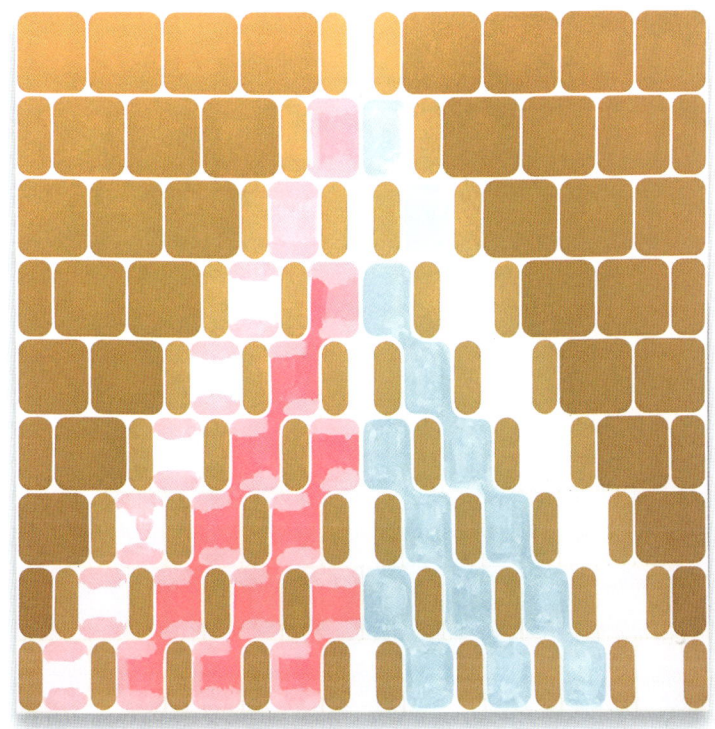
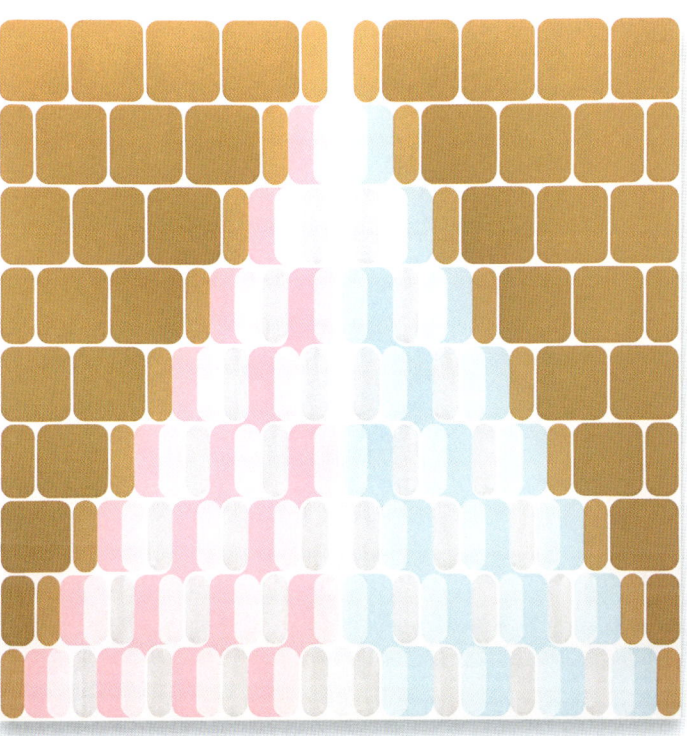

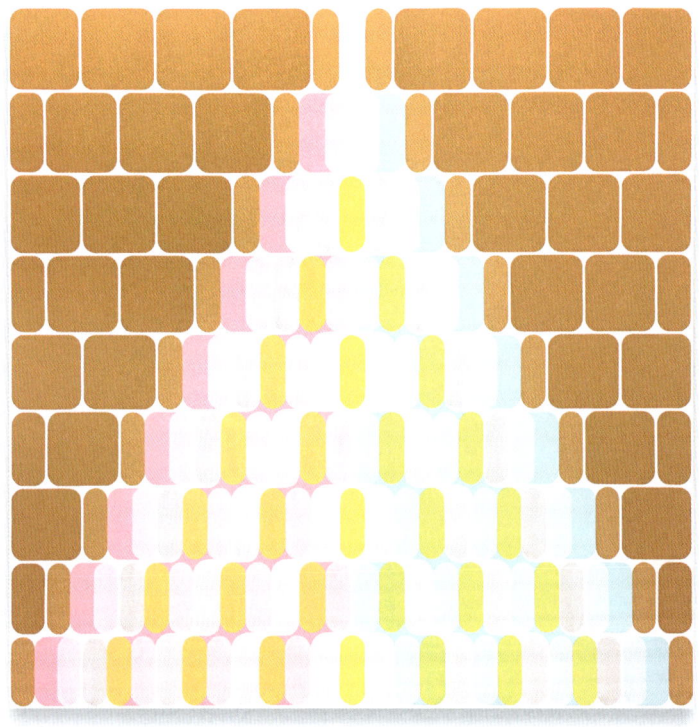
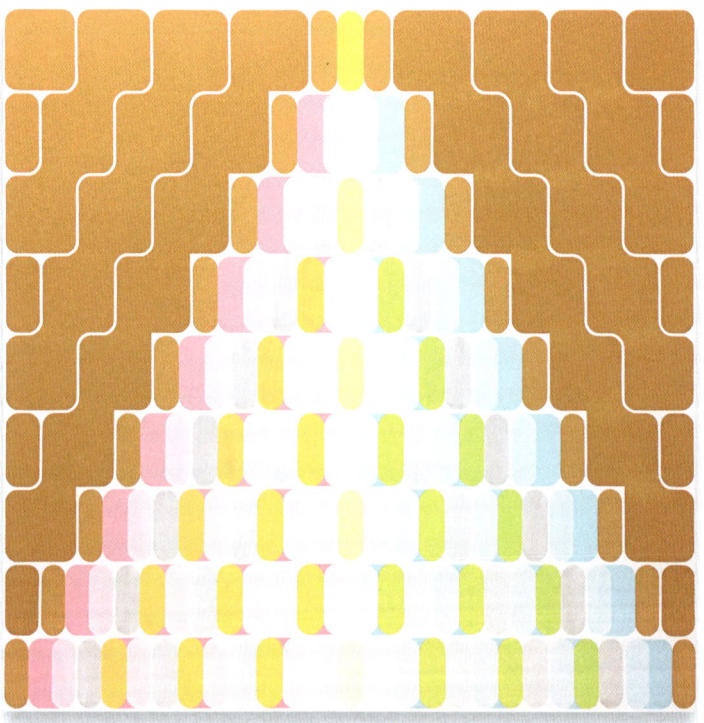

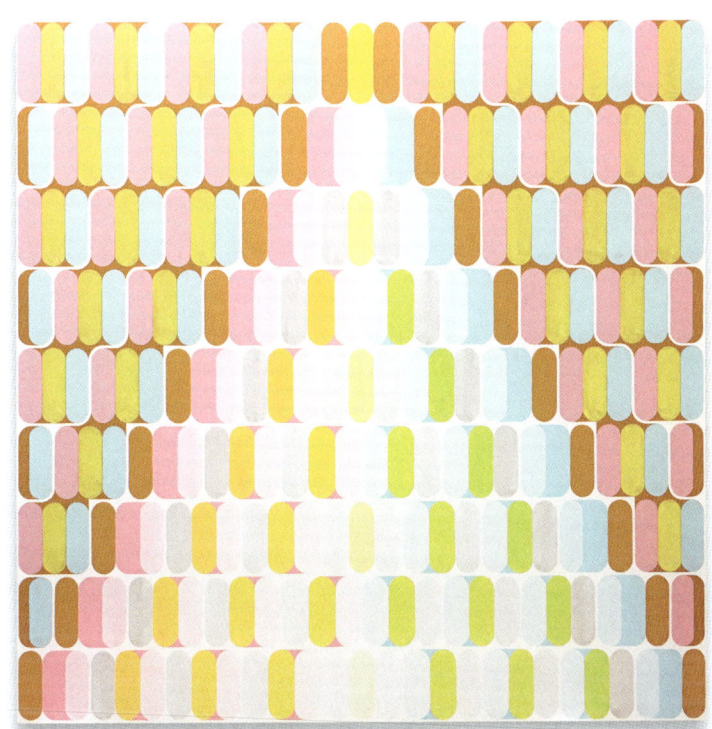
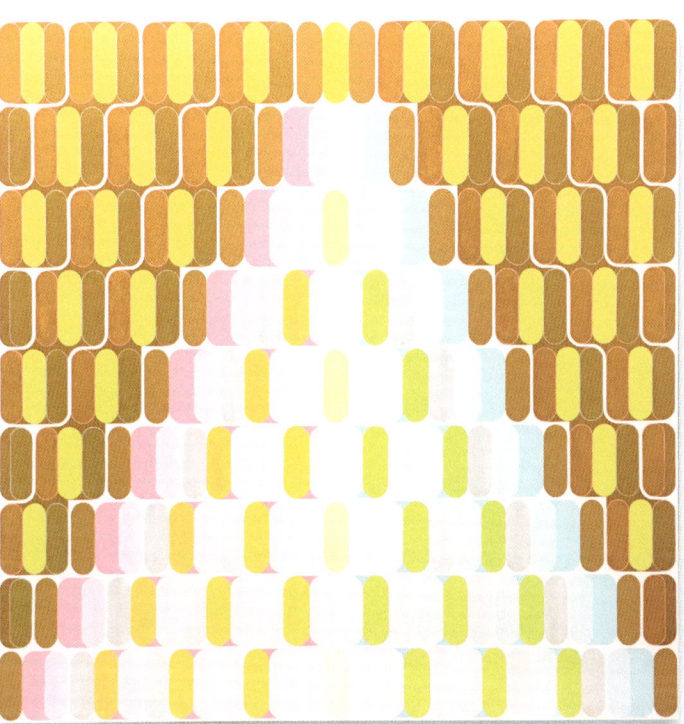

May 15, 2021

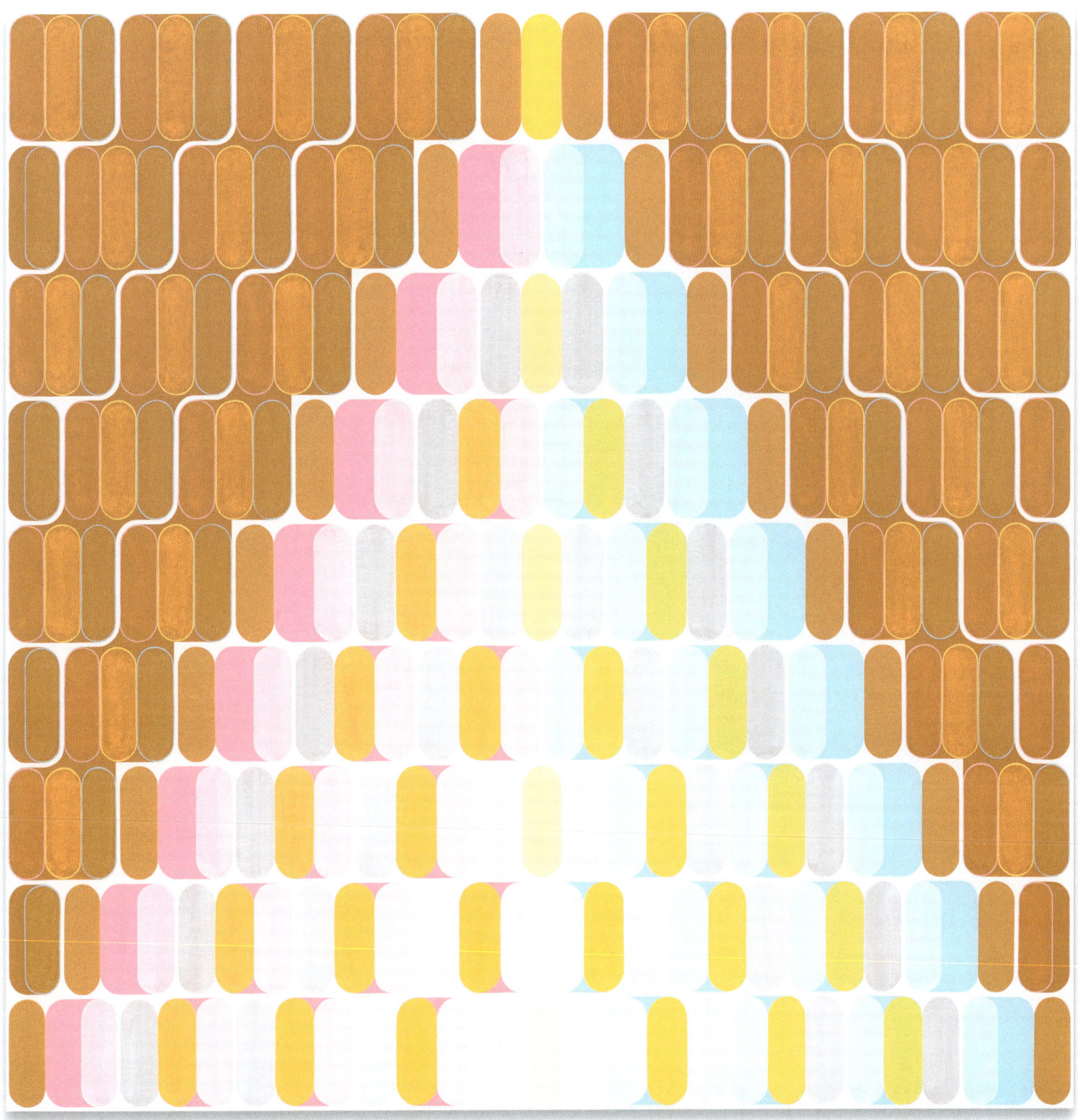

Vent, 2021, acrylic on canvas, 70×70 inches / 177.8×177.8 cm

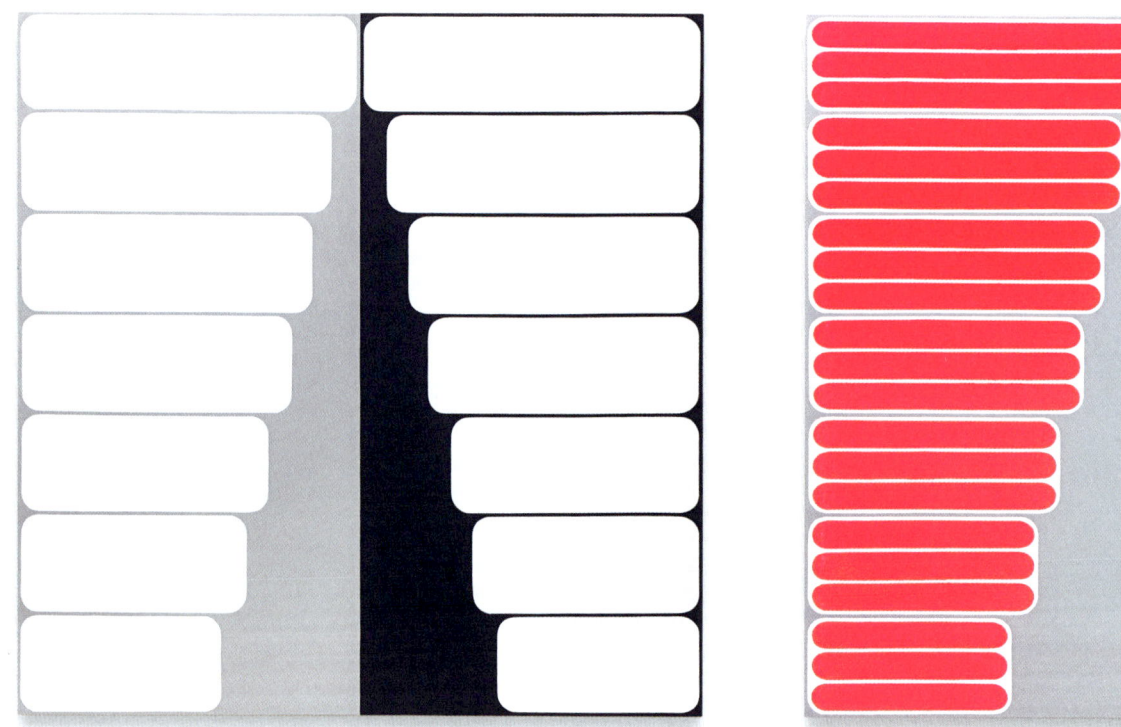

November 15, 2021

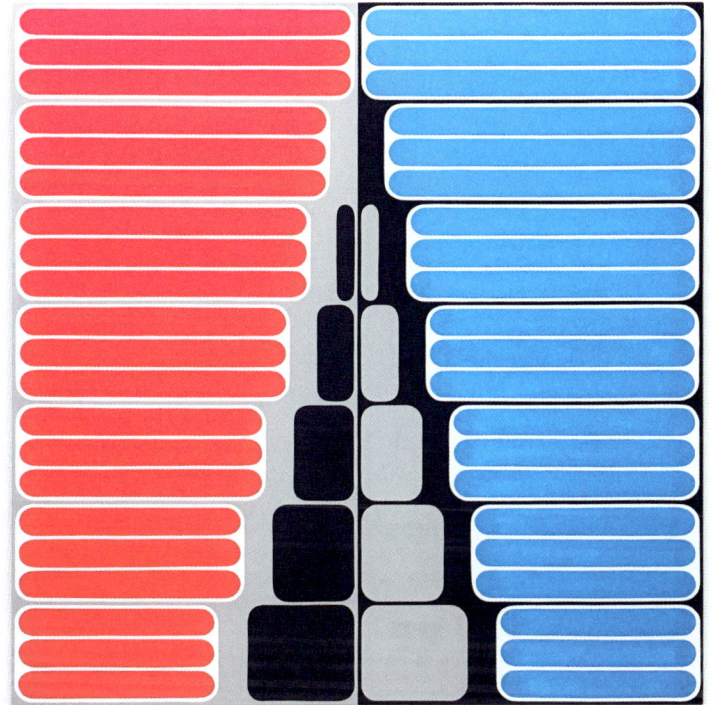

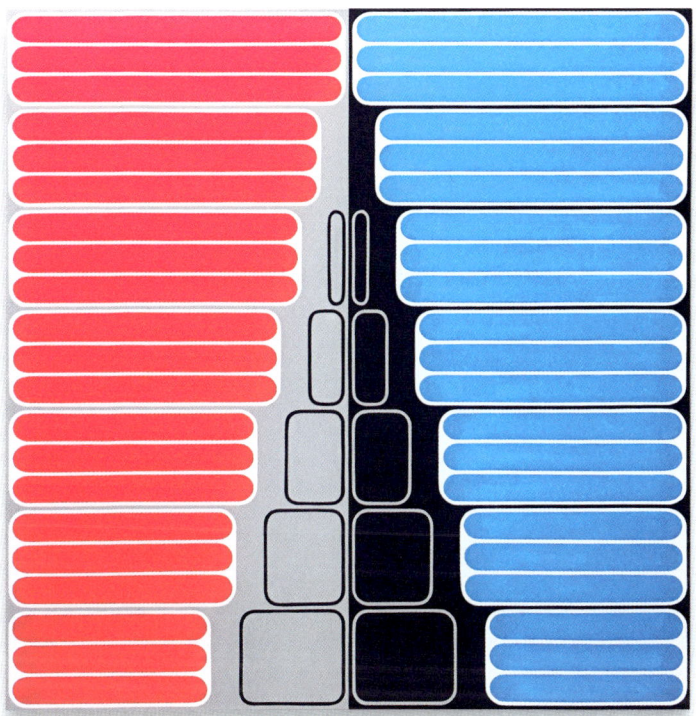

December 10, 2021

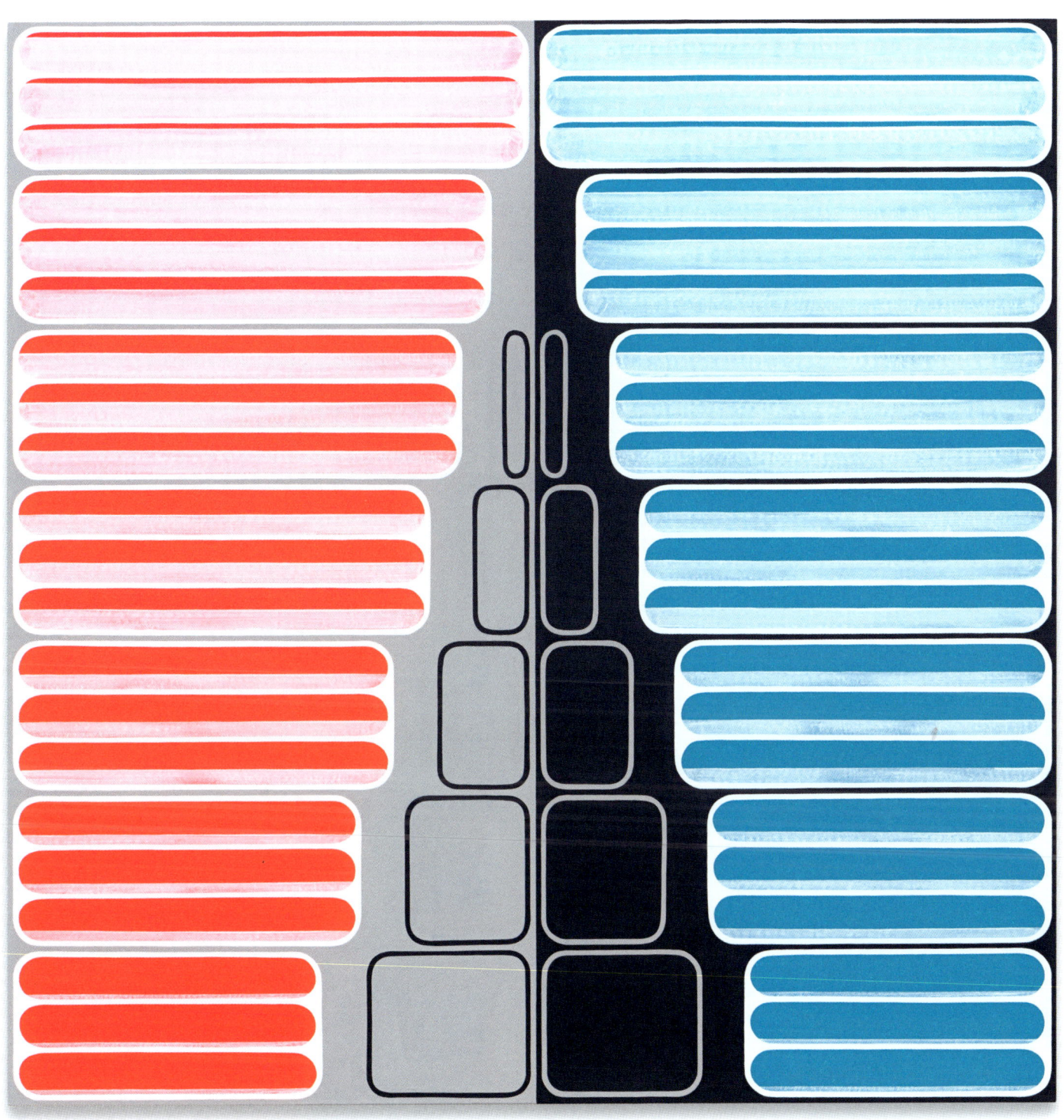

Construct, 2021, acrylic on canvas, 55×55 inches / 139.7×139.7 cm

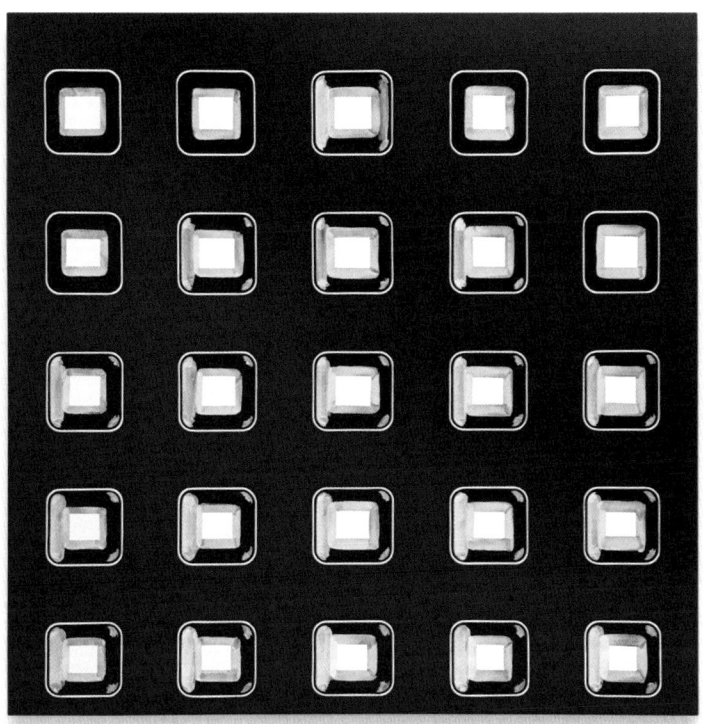

June 6, 2021

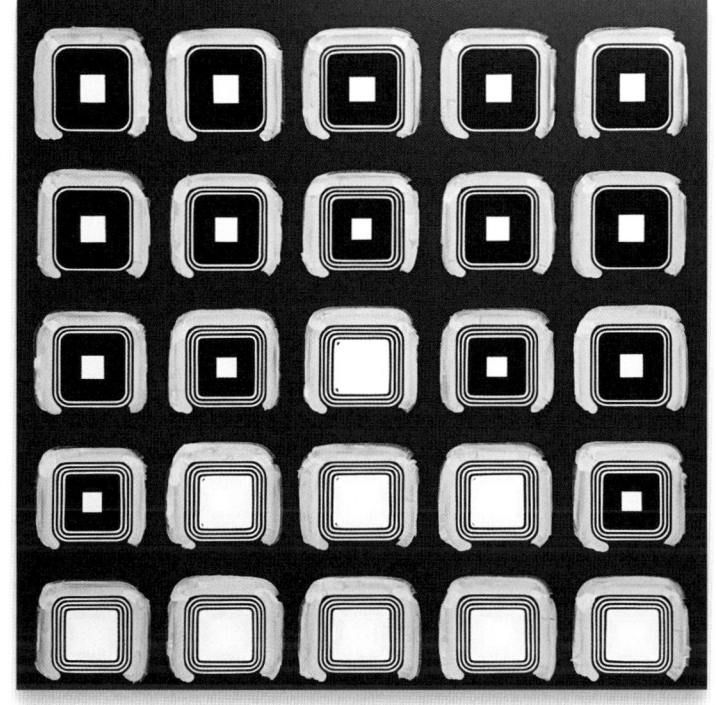
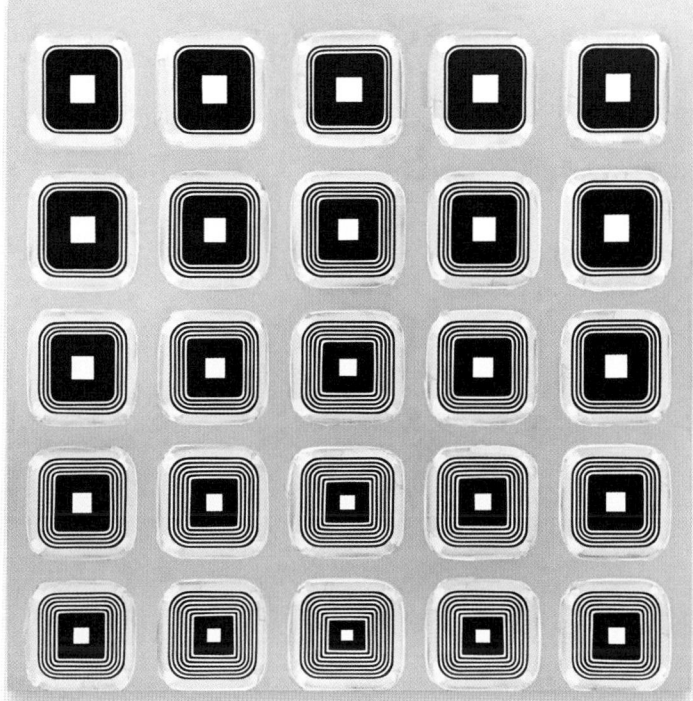

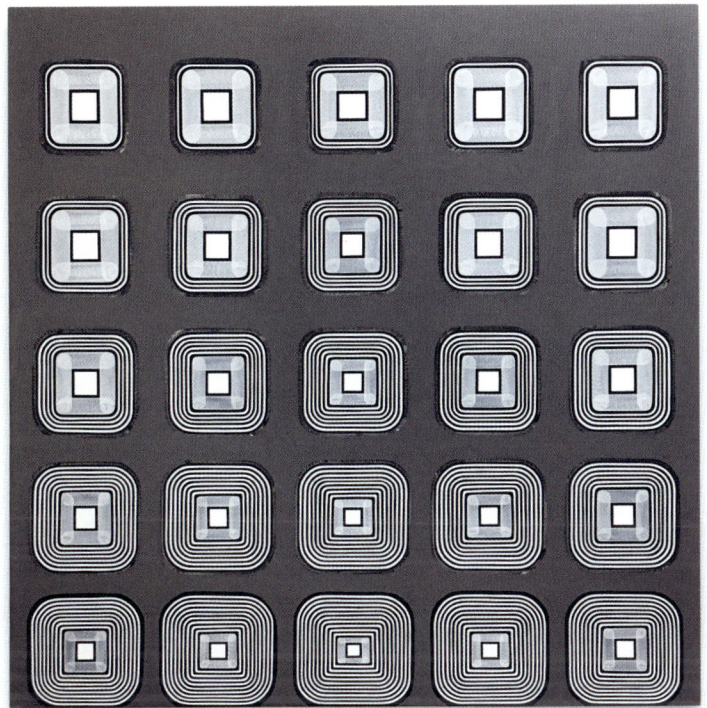
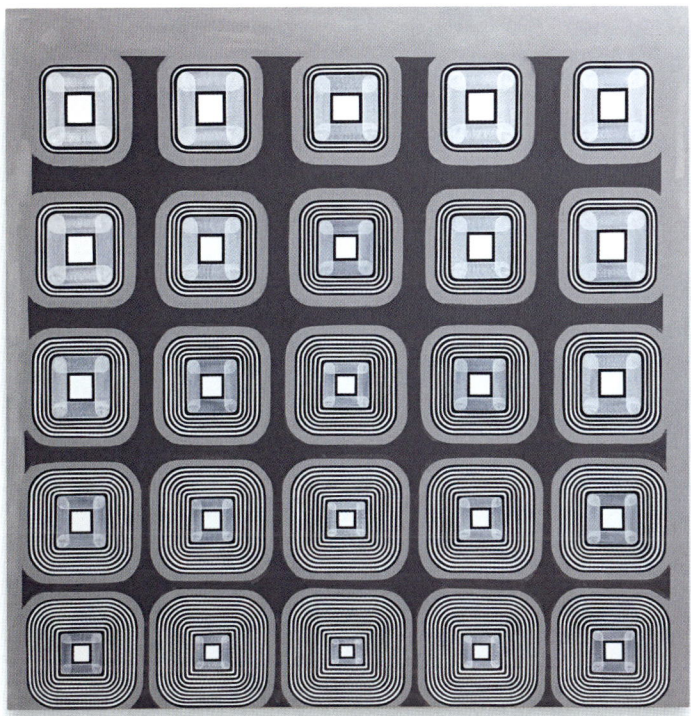

August 1, 2021

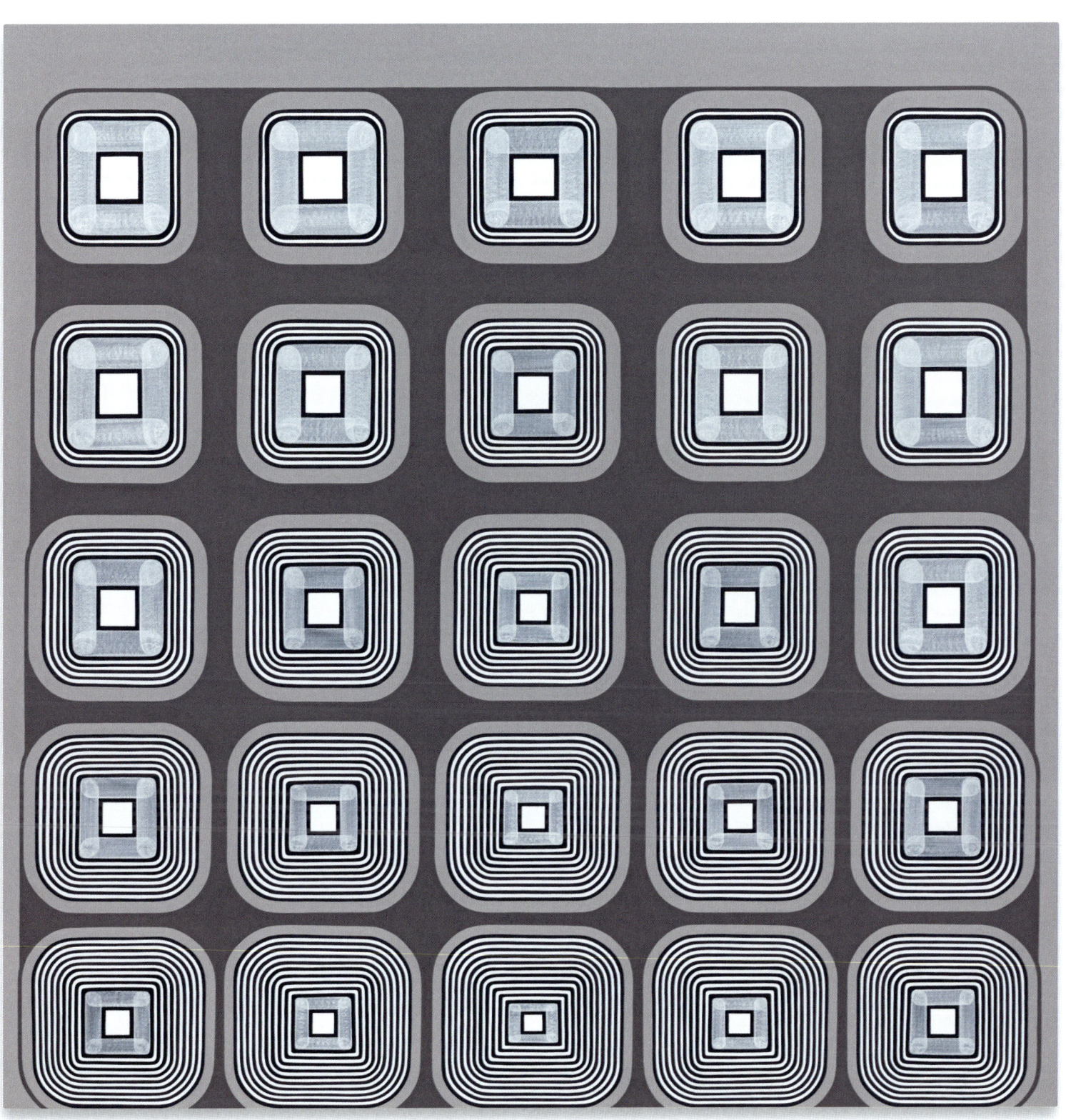

Outlet, 2021, acrylic on canvas, 70×70 inches / 177.8×177.8 cm

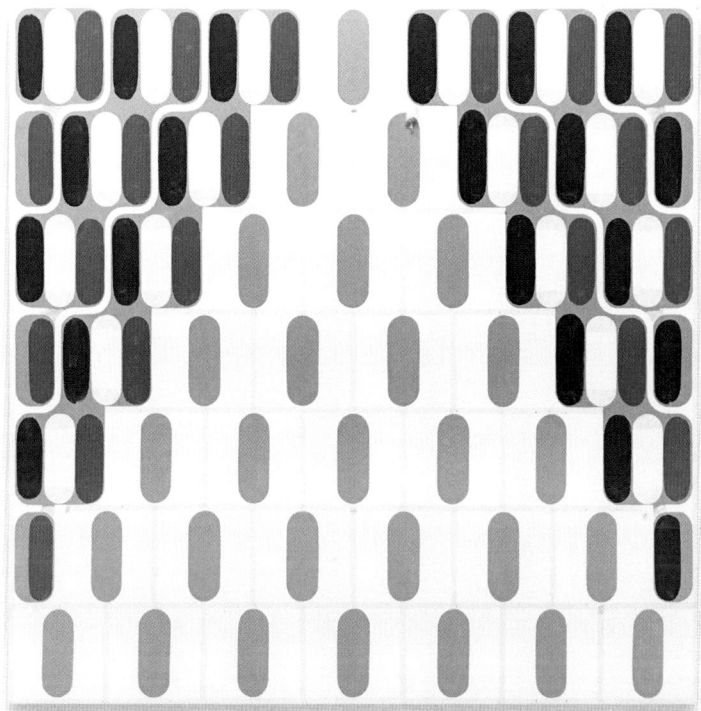

February 23, 2022

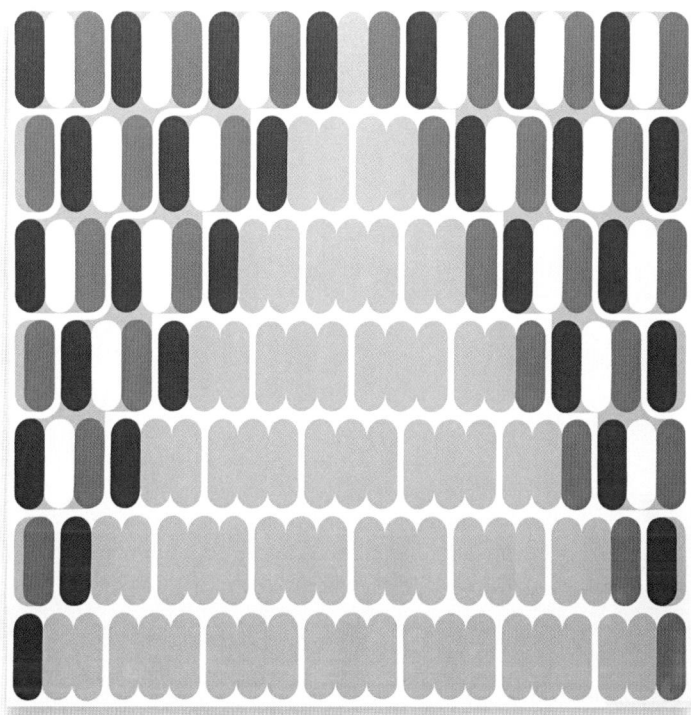

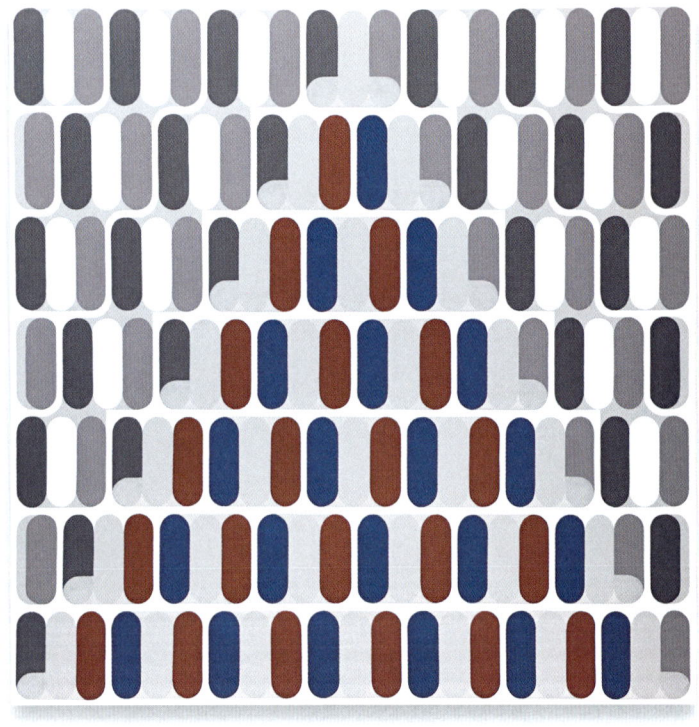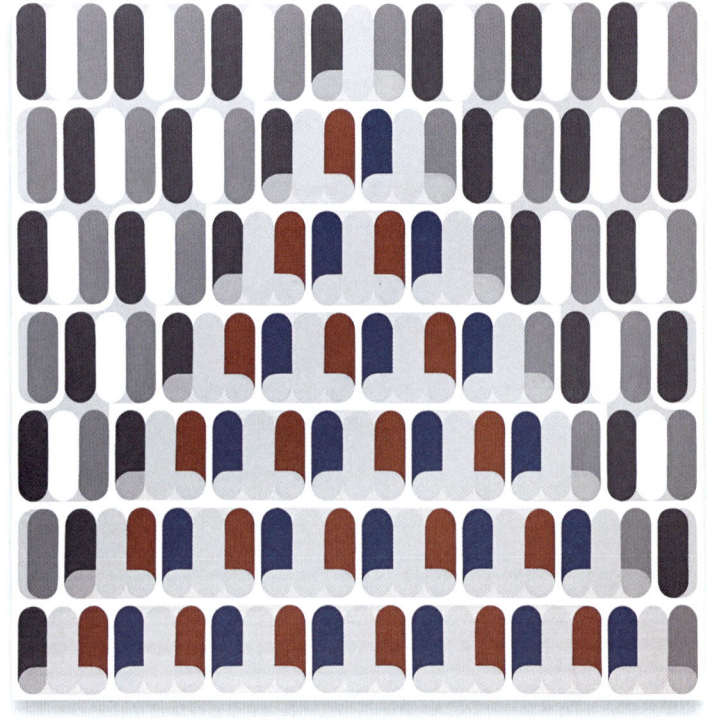

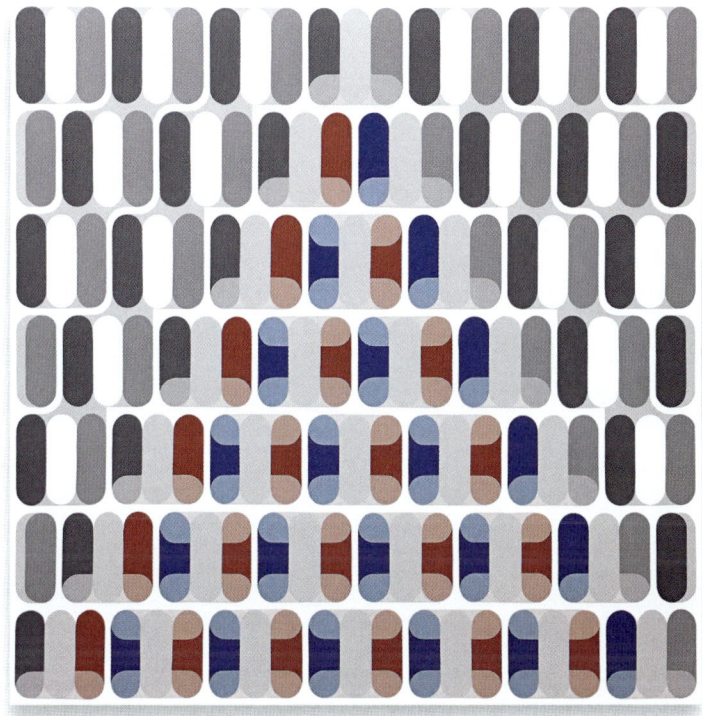

March 9, 2022

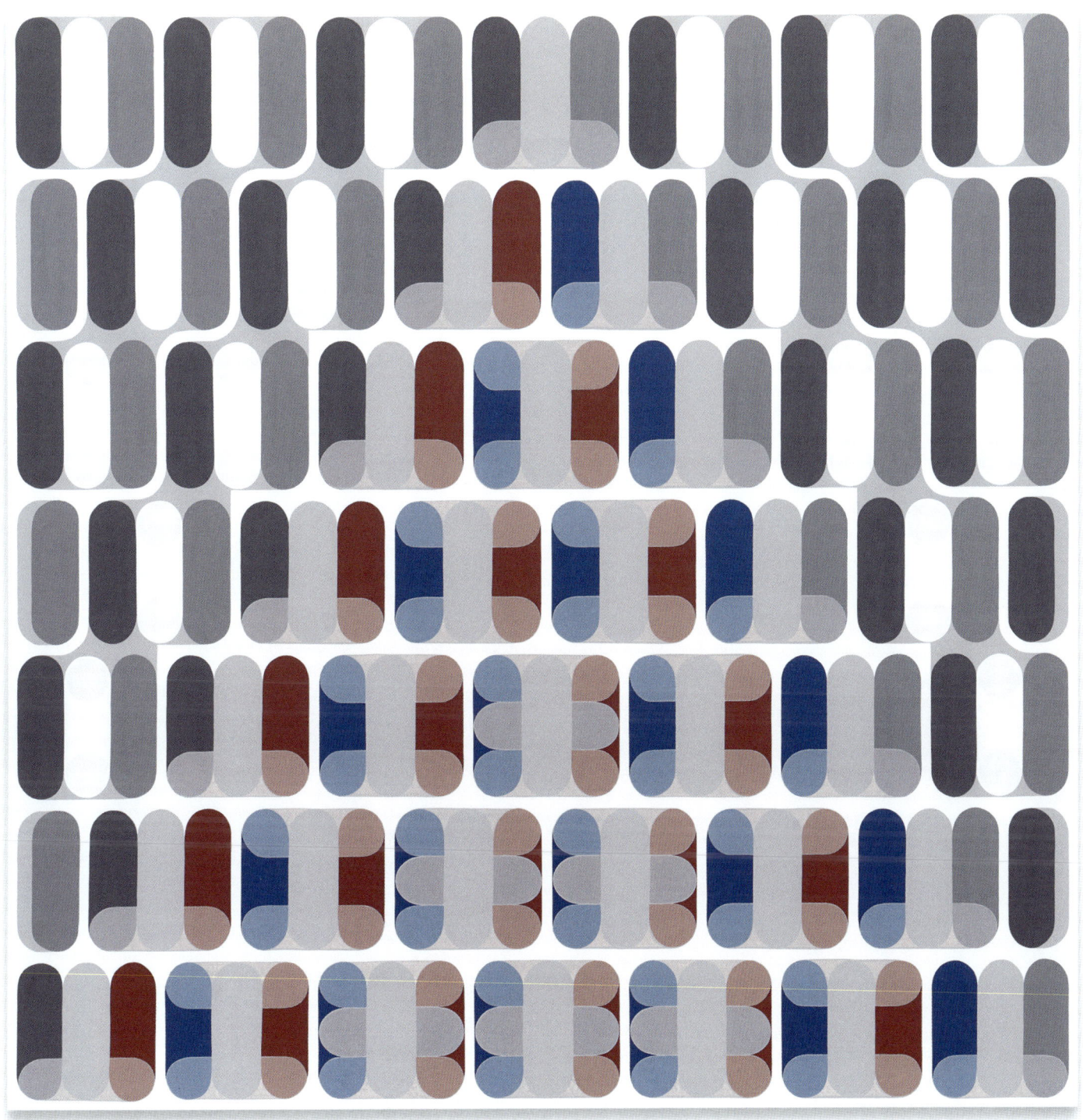

Demand, 2022, acrylic on canvas, 55×55 inches / 139.7×139.7 cm

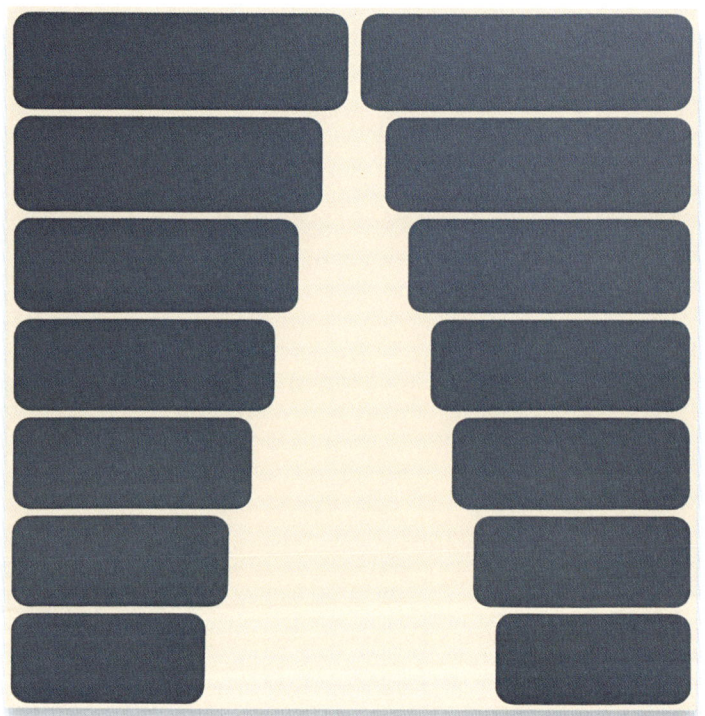

March 23, 2022

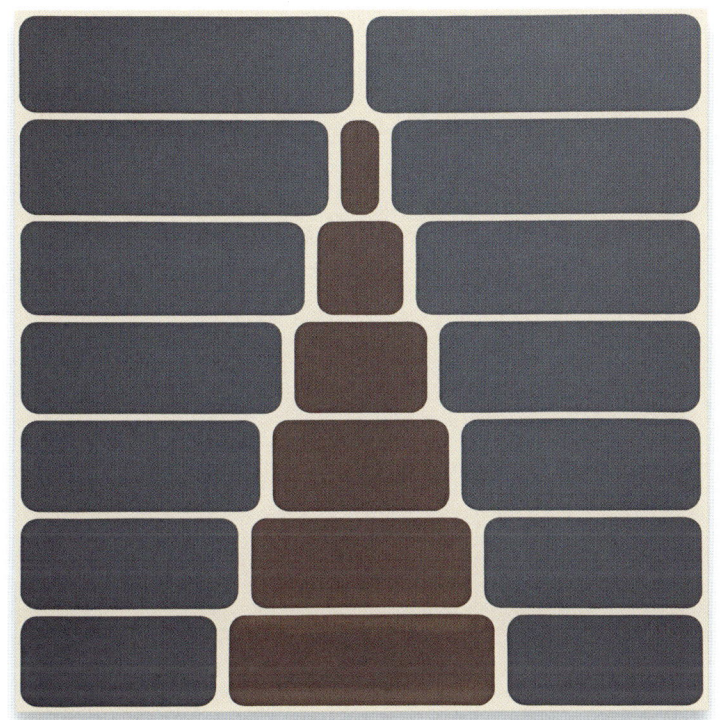 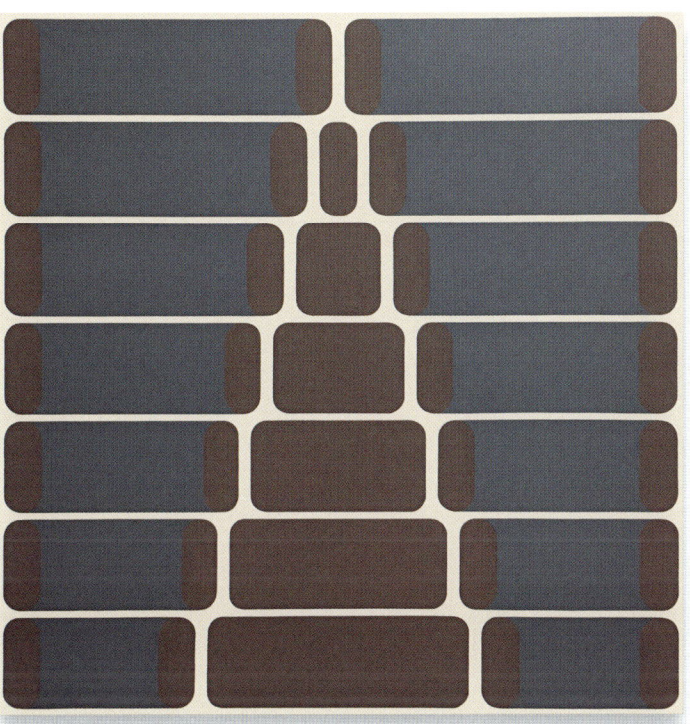

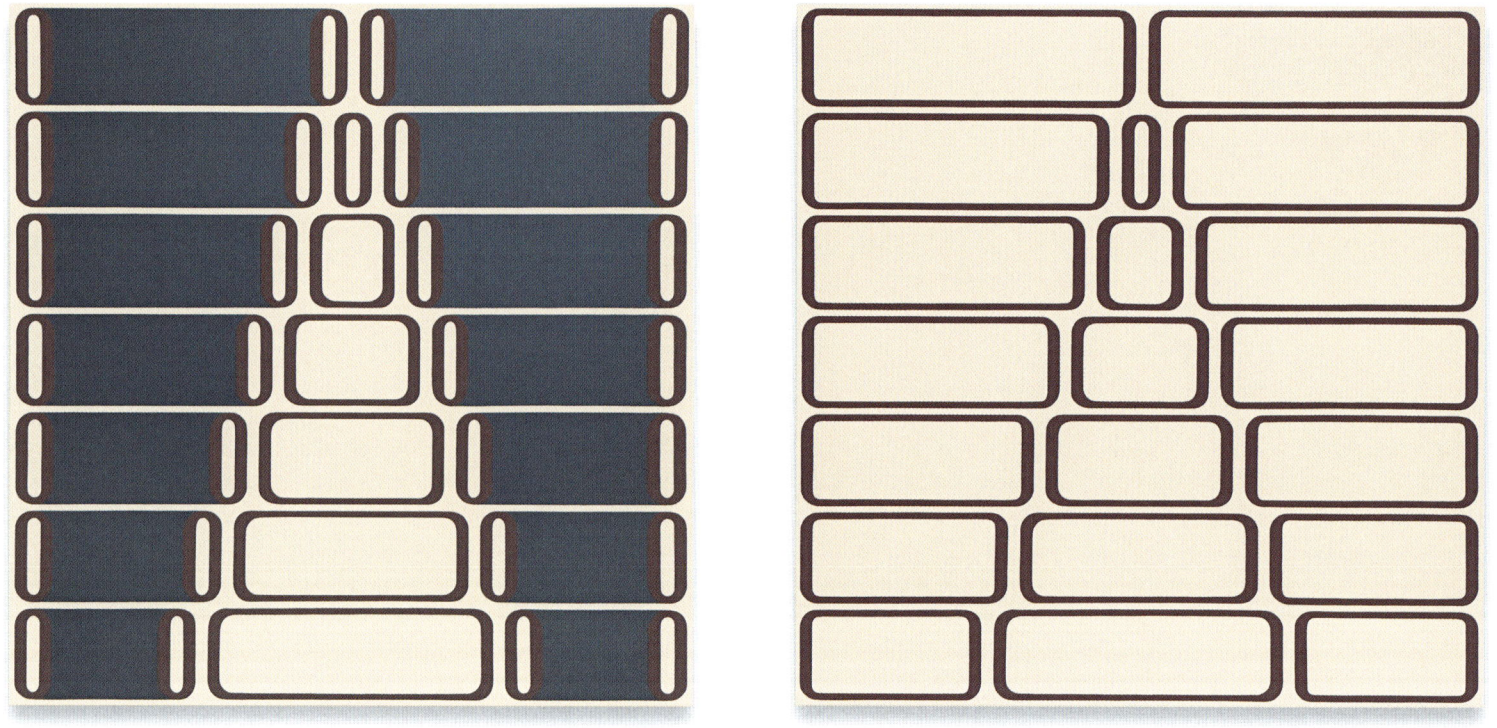

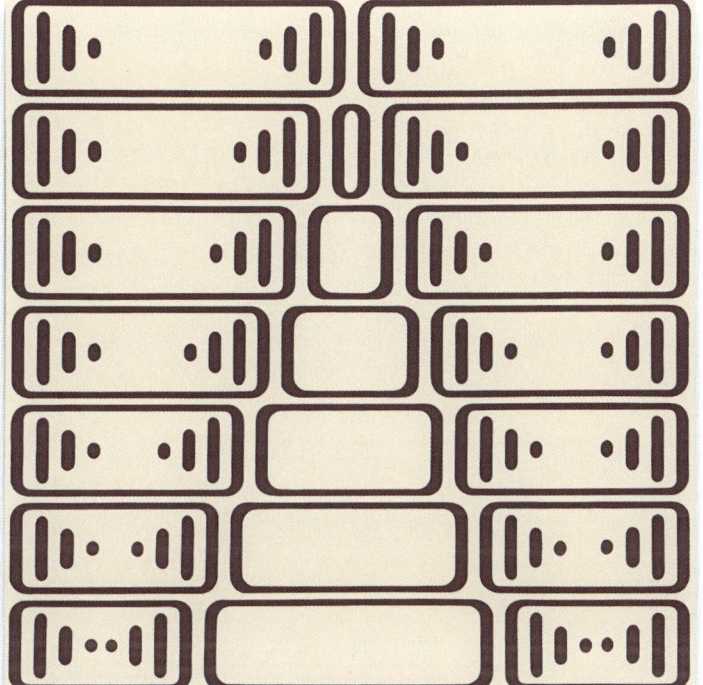
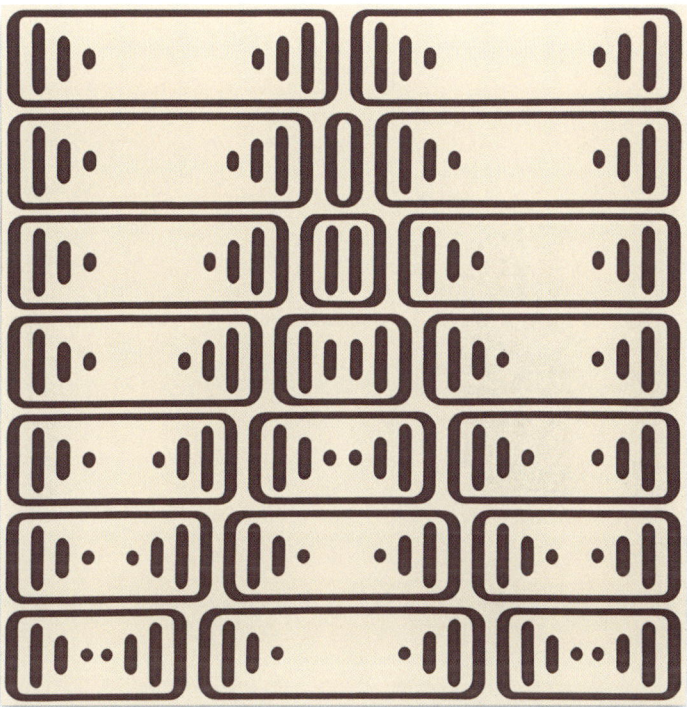

April 19, 2022

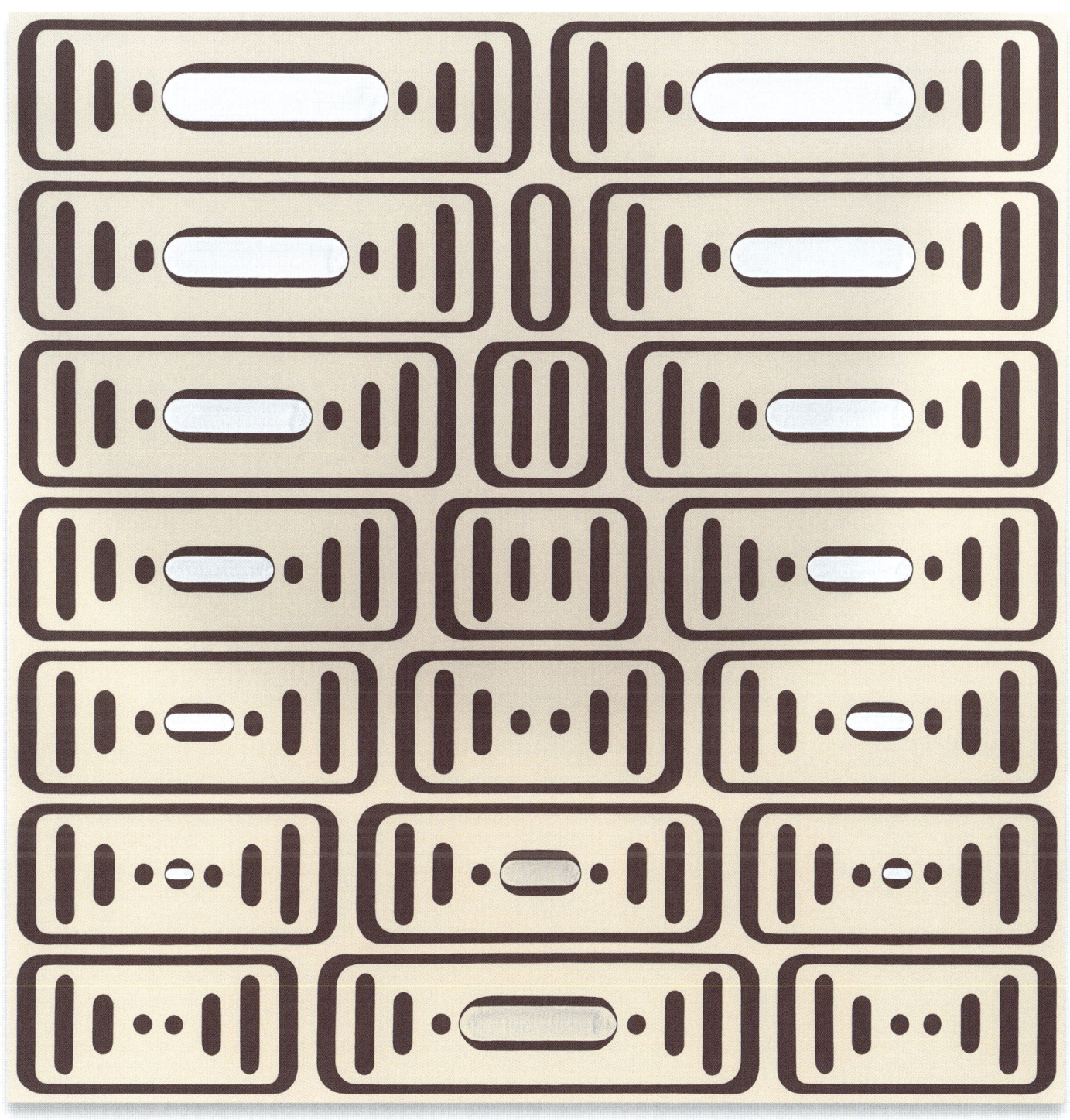

Call, 2022, acrylic on canvas, 55×55 inches/139.7×139.7 cm

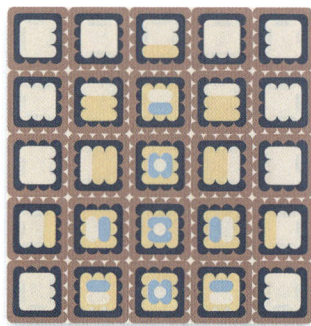

Gate, 2019
Acrylic on canvas
55×55 inches
139.7×139.7 cm

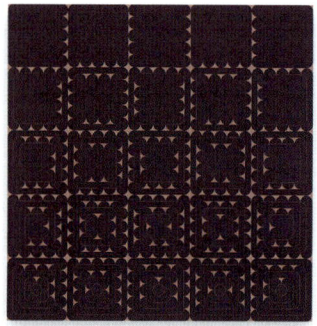

Waive, 2019
Acrylic on canvas
55×55 inches
139.7×139.7 cm

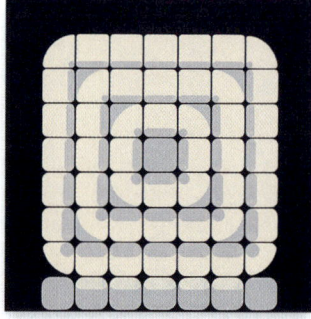

Compound, 2019
Acrylic on canvas
55×55 inches
139.7×139.7 cm

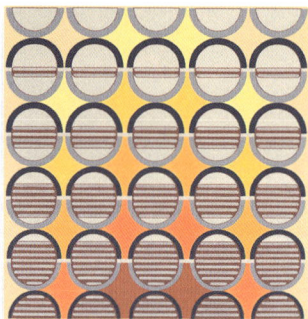

Eclipse, 2020
Acrylic on canvas
55×55 inches
139.7×139.7 cm

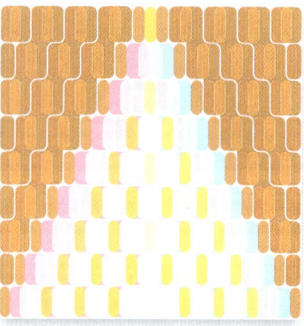

Vent, 2021
Acrylic on canvas
70×70 inches
177.8×177.8 cm

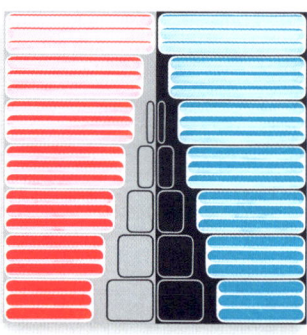

Construct, 2021
Acrylic on canvas
55×55 inches
139.7×139.7 cm

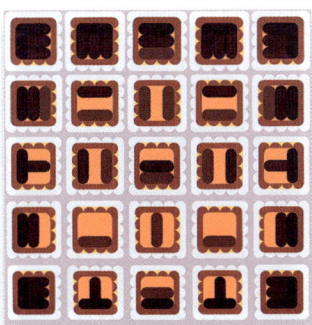

Score, 2020
Acrylic on canvas
70×70 inches
177.8×177.8 cm

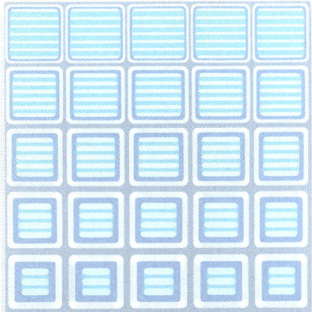

Wake, 2020
Acrylic on canvas
55×55 inches
139.7×139.7 cm

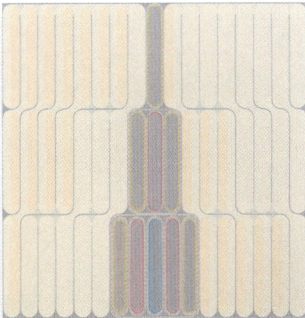

Prime, 2020
Acrylic on canvas
55×55 inches
139.7×139.7 cm

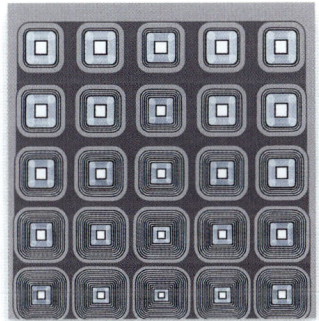

Outlet, 2021
Acrylic on canvas
70×70 inches
177.8×177.8 cm

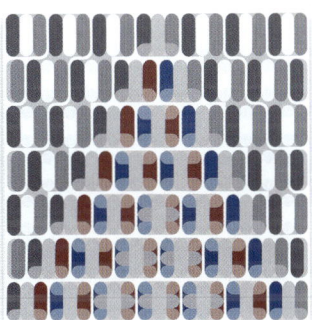

Demand, 2022
Acrylic on canvas
55×55 inches
139.7×139.7 cm

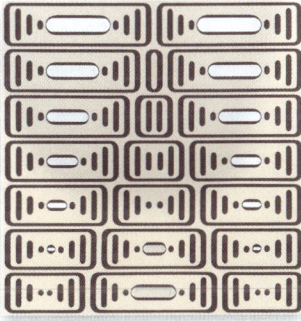

Call, 2022
Acrylic on canvas
55×55 inches
139.7×139.7 cm

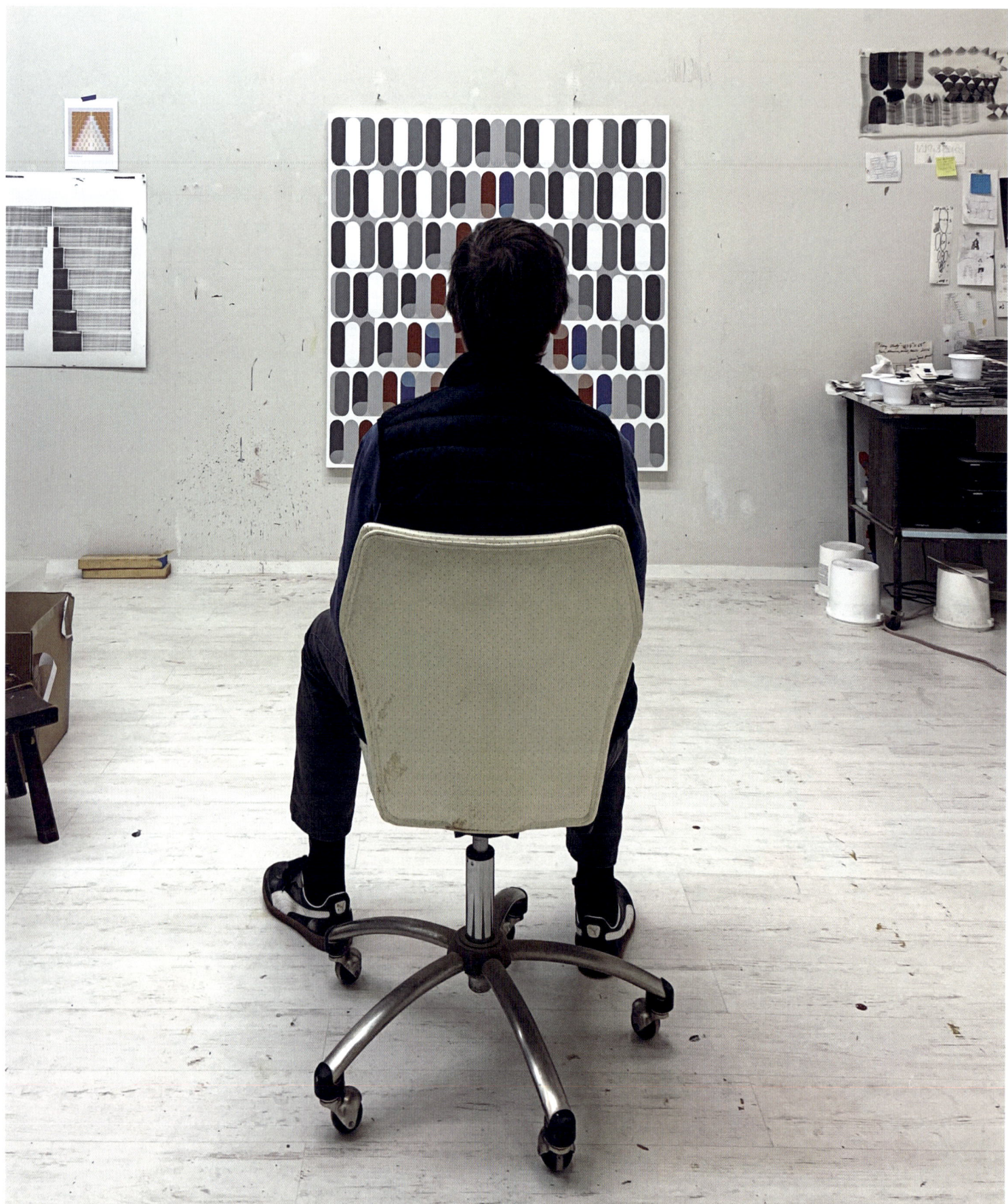

Dan Walsh (b. 1960, Philadelphia, Pennsylvania) is a painter, printmaker, bookmaker, and sculptor. Rooted in a meditative geometry, his work explores the boundaries of abstraction through subtly irregular shapes, inconstant lines, and a pervasive wit. Walsh's work has been exhibited in venues throughout the U.S. and Europe, including The Museum of Modern Art and the New Museum, New York; the Centre National d'Art Contemporain, Nice; the Rhode Island School of Design Art Museum, Providence; and the Musée d'Art Moderne et Contemporain, Geneva, Switzerland. He has also been included in the Ljubljana Biennial, Slovenia, the Lyon Biennial of Contemporary Art, France, and the Whitney Biennial, New York (2014). In 2019, his work was the subject of a 10-year retrospective at the Bonnefantenmuseum in Maastricht. He is represented in the collections of The Museum of Modern Art, New York; the Art Institute of Chicago; the Jumex Collection, Mexico City; and the Musée d'Art Moderne et Contemporain in Geneva, among other institutions. In October 2022, Walsh was inducted into the National Academy of Design.

Dan Walsh
The Process of Painting

Editorial Work
Clément Dirié, Clare Manchester

Author
Bob Nickas

Graphic Design & Production
Peter Willberg, London

Typeface
Van Condensed

Jacket
Dan Walsh Studio, New York, 2022

Photo Credits
All images by Dan Walsh,
except p. 21, 27, 33, 41, 49, 57,
63, 69, 73, 79, 85, 91: courtesy
Paula Cooper Gallery, New York;
and p. 94: Kristin Ordahl

Color Separation & Print
Printmanagment Plitt GmbH,
Oberhausen (Germany)

Acknowledgments
Dan Walsh would like to thank
Elsbeth Bisig Tschudi, Peter Willberg,
Bob Nickas, Kristin Ordahl,
Martita Slewe, Paula Cooper,
Anthony Allen, and Laura Tiozzo.

Published by
JRP|Editions
Rue des Bains, 39
CH–1205 Geneva
www.jrp-editions.com

in collaboration with
Galerie Tschudi, Zuoz/Zurich
www.galerie-tschudi.ch

ISBN: 978-3-03764-607-6
Printed in Europe.

JRP|Editions publications are available
internationally at selected bookstores
and from the following distribution
partners:

Switzerland | AVA Verlagsauslieferung AG
ava.ch

Germany and Austria | By JRP|Editions
jrp-editions.com

France | Les presses du réel
lespressesdureel.com

UK and other European countries |
Cornerhouse Publications, HOME
cornerhousepublications.org

USA, Canada, Asia and Australia |
ARTBOOK|D.A.P.
artbook.com

For a list of our partner bookshops
or for any general questions, please
contact JRP|Editions directly at
info@jrp-editions.com, or visit our
homepage jrp-editions.com for further
information about our program.